Nita Mehta's **101**

Vegetarian
recipes

Nita Mehta's # 101
Vegetarian
recipes

Nita Mehta

B.Sc. (Home Science)
M.Sc. (Food and Nutrition), Gold Medalist

Co-Author
Anu Kshetrapal

Nita Mehta's 101 Vegetarian recipes

First Hardbound Edition 2008

ISBN 978-81-7869-212-8

Food Styling & Photography: *Tanya Mehta*

Layout and laser typesetting:

National Information
Technology Academy
3A/3, Asaf Ali Road
New Delhi-110 002
☎ 23252948

Published by:

SNAB
Publishers Pvt. Ltd.
3A/3 Asaf Ali Road,
New Delhi - 110002
Tel: 23252948, 23250091
Telefax:91-11-23250091

Editorial and Marketing office:
E-159, Greater Kailash-II, N.Delhi-48
Fax: 91-11-29225218, 29229558
Tel: 91-11-29214011, 29218727, 29218574
E-Mail: nitamehta@email.com
   nitamehta@nitamehta.com
   *Website:*http://www.nitamehta.com
   Website: http://www.snabindia.com

Printed at:
Paras Offset Pvt.Ltd., C-176, Naraina Phase-1
New Delhi-110028

Distributed by:
THE VARIETY BOOK DEPOT
A.V.G. Bhavan, M 3 Con Circus
New Delhi - 110 001
Tel: 23417175, 23412567; Fax: 23415335
E-mail: varietybookdepot@rediffmail.com

Contributing Writers :
Anurag Mehta
Tanya Mehta
Editorial & Proofreading :
Rakesh
Ramesh

Price: Rs. 250/-

Introduction

Vegetarian eating is a healthy alternative for today's life-style. The recipes in this book provide delectable dishes which can be combined, or can be enjoyed as a hearty meal on their own. Influenced by cuisines from around the world, there are easy-to-prepare dishes which have the wonderful texture and flavour of fresh vegetables.

The book carries 101 recipes ranging from appetizers to desserts. The main course has Indian as well as Continental dishes. The fusion stir fries are quick recipes which can be assembled for unexpected guests or when you are short of time. *Raitas*, breads and rice will make the meal complete.

We have seen to it that all recipes have a distinct flavour and texture of their own. We now have such a vast variety of spices, herbs and sauces available and each imparts a special taste. Recipes have been tried several times, till we were fully satisfied with the final product. Just follow the steps and we are sure you will get loads of appreciation from family and friends.

Enjoy!

Nita Mehta

Contents

Steaming Soups   36

Gourmet Salads   42

Tantalizing Taste of Raitas   48

Fusion Stir-Fries   51

Continental Cuisine 58

Fun with Indian *Kadhai* & Handi 76

Rice & Paranthas   100

Delectable Desserts   109

Drinks & Smoothie Treats

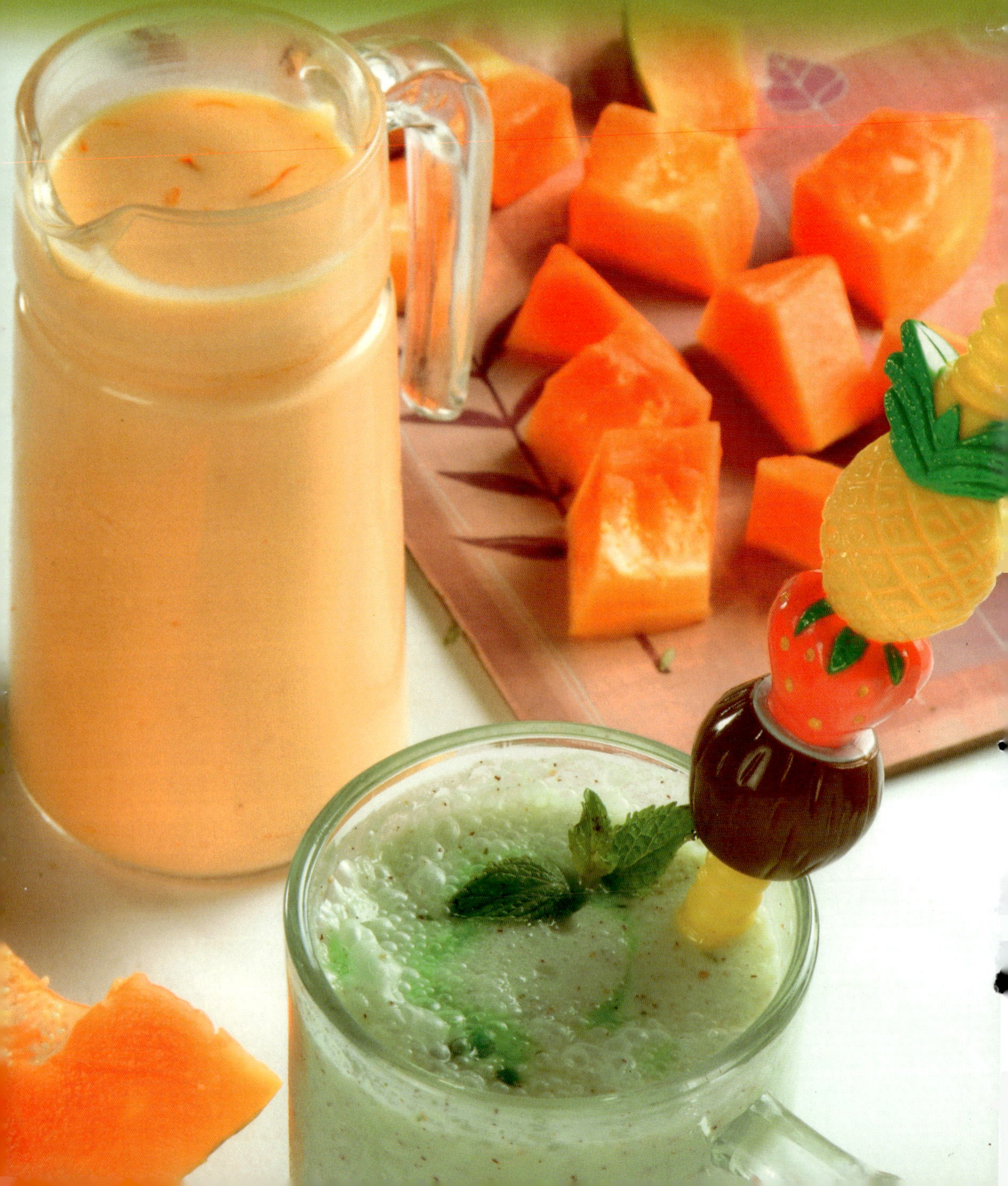

Smoothie Bar

To make a smoothie all the ingredient should be chilled as ice is not added to a smoothie. Place all the ingredients ½ hour before in the freezer.

PAPAYA HONEY SMOOTHIE

Serves 2

1 cup chopped papaya, ½ cup cold milk, 1 cup thick yogurt, ½ cup vanilla ice cream
1 tbsp honey, few strands saffron (*kesar*) - soaked in 1 tbsp of warm milk

1. Put papaya and milk in a blender and blend till smooth.
2. Add all the remaining ingredients and blend until thick and frothy. Serve cold.

STRAWBERRY ALMOND SMOOTHIE

Serves 2

1 cup chopped strawberries, 2 tbsp powdered sugar
1 cup fresh thick yogurt, 1 cup cold milk, 4 tbsp strawberry ice cream

GARNISH
1 tbsp almonds - toasted and crushed, few strawberries - chopped

1. Mix strawberries and sugar and blend until smooth.
2. Add all the other ingredients and blend until thick and frothy. Serve chilled topped with almonds and strawberries.

KIWI MINT SMOOTHIE

Serves 2

1 soft, ripe kiwi - chopped finely, 2 tbsp mint leaves, 4 tbsp khus syrup
4 tbsp vanilla ice cream, 1 cup cold milk, 1 cup limca or sprite

1. Blend kiwi, mint leaves and khus khus syrup in a blender till smooth.
2. Add ice cream and milk to the blender and blend again. Pour into 2 glasses.
3. Top with some limca or sprite. Serve garnished with mint.

BLACK CURRANT DELIGHT

Serves 1

3 tbsp black currant crush
1 tbsp cream
½ cup chilled milk
2 tbsp chopped fresh pineapple or mango
2 tbsp crushed ice

1. Blend crush, cream, milk and fruit together in a mixer.

2. Put some ice in the glass. Pour the drink over the ice. Top with a few drops of crush on the top too if you like. Serve with a straw.

PINEAPPLE & LICHI MELODY

Serves 1

2 slices fresh pineapple - cut into 1" pieces
2 tbsp sugar, or to taste
6-8 leaves mint (*poodina*)
¼ tsp black salt
¾ cup lichi juice
pinch of freshly crushed pepper
8-10 cubes of ice

1. Heat a non stick pan, sprinkle sugar on it. Place the pineapple pieces in the pan and cook till sugar caramelizes and pineapples turn slightly soft. Add ¼ cup water, bring to a boil. Cool.

2. In a blender pour the pineapples along-with caramelized water, mint, salt, pepper and lichi juice.

3. Add ice cubes and liquidize till smooth. Add some powdered sugar if you like it sweeter. Pour in a glass and garnish with mint.

PLUM COOLER

Serves 6 -8

½ kg firm plums (*aloo bukhara*)
6 cups water, ½ cup sugar
4 tbsp strawberry crush
1 tsp rock salt (*kala namak*)
few fresh mint leaves (*poodina*)

1. Wash the plums and chop them into large pieces to deseed the plums. Place the chopped plums in a pressure cooker, add 6 cups water and pressure-cook to give 2 whistles. Remove from heat. When pressure drops open the lid, and add the sugar to the hot mixture. Mix well to dissolve sugar. Let it cool.

2. Place the mixture in a blender and blend till smooth. Strain the mixture.

3. Add strawberry crush and salt and roughly chopped mint leaves to the plum juice. Check sugar and add some powdered sugar if needed. Chill.

4. To serve, place a few ice cubes in a glass, pour the cooler. Decorate with mint.

MINTY LEMONADE

Serves 2

½ lemon - wash & cut into 4 pieces
¼ cup sugar syrup (boil ¼ cup sugar with ¼ cup water and cool)
¼ tsp salt, a pinch of black salt, ½ cup chilled water
6-7 cubes of ice, ¼ cup chilled soda

GARNISH
2-4 fresh or tinned cherries
2 tbsp mint leaves - very finely chopped
a pinch of black pepper

1. Blend lemon pieces with sugar syrup, salt, black salt, ½ cup cold water in a blender. Strain.

2. Put lemon-sugar syrup in a glass.

3. Put ice in the glass.

4. Add mint and cherries.

5. Top with soda and a pinch of black pepper.

FRUIT PUNCH

Serves 2

½ cup orange juice
½ cup pineapple juice
½ cup mango juice
3 tbsp fresh cream
½ tsp grenadine syrup, optional

GARNISH (FRUITY STIRRER)
balls of watermelon, black grapes and mint leaves

1. Thread watermelon balls and grapes with mint leaves in between on a wooden skewer to make a fruity stirrer and keep aside.

2. Blend all the juices and cream together. Add a few drops of grenadine and blend again.

3. Put crushed ice in a glass. Pour the punch mixture on top.

4. Put the prepared stirrer in the glass. Serve.

Quick & Tasty Snacks

ALOO METHI KI TIKKI

Boiled potatoes combined with fenugreek greens.

Makes 10-12

½ kg (5-6) potatoes - boiled & mashed finely
1 cup fenugreek greens (*methi*) - chopped very finely
3 tbsp oil, 1 tsp cumin seeds (*jeera*)
1 onion - chopped finely, 2 green chillies - chopped finely
¼ tsp turmeric (*haldi*), 1 tsp cumin (*jeera*) powder, 1 tsp salt, ½ tsp garam masala
¼ cup chopped coriander
2 tbsp dry fenugreek leaves (*kasoori methi*) - roast on a *tawa* for 2 minutes and crushed
2 bread slices - grind in a mixer to get fresh crumbs
oil for frying, chat masala to sprinkle

1. Heat oil in a *kadhai*, add cumin. Stir and add onion and green chillies. Stir-fry till onions turn transparent. Add fenugreek greens. Add turmeric, cumin powder, salt, garam masala, coriander leaves. Mix well. Cook for 4-5 minutes till almost dry.

2. Add potatoes and dry fenugreek leaves. Mix for 2 minutes. Remove from fire.

3. Add the bread crumbs. Mix well and shape into round flat tikkis. Keep aside for ½ hour to set properly. Fry till golden brown, remove on paper towel to remove excess oil. Sprinkle *chaat masala*. Serve hot.

VEGGIE CHEESE SLICE

Serves 6-8

1 small french loaf or bread, 2 tbsp butter

TOPPING
¾ cup grated cheddar cheese, 2 tbsp finely chopped onions
2 tbsp finely chopped capsicum
2 tbsp finely chopped deseeded tomato (cut a tomato into 4 pieces and remove pulp)
2 tbsp corn kernels, 1 tbsp olive oil or cream
4-5 fresh basil leaves - roughly torn or 2 tbsp chopped coriander
½ tsp chilli flakes, ½ tsp oregano, ¼ tsp pepper, a pinch of salt, 1 tsp mustard paste

1. Cut the french bread into 1" thick diagonal slices. Apply butter and grill with the buttered side up till golden brown.

2. Mix all the ingredients of the topping lightly in a bowl. Pile the topping on the untoasted side of the bread. Place bread under a grill for 3-4 minutes and grill till cheese melts. Serve immediately.

CRISPY CAULIFLOWER KOTHEY

Balls with Chinese flavourings. Mix kothey to the sauce only at the time of serving as the sauce will make the kothey soggy.

Makes 12

2 cups very finely chopped cauliflower (minced)
2 slices bread
2 tbsp plain flour (*maida*), 2 tbsp cornflour
½ tbsp rice flour, optional
1 tsp chilli powder, ½ tsp pepper powder, ½ tsp salt
pinch of baking soda (*mitha soda*)
oil for frying

KOTHEY SAUCE
1 tbsp oil
12 flakes garlic - finely chopped (1 tbsp)
1 small onion - finely chopped, 1 small capsicum - finely chopped
¼ cup hot sweet sauce or tomato ketchup
½ tsp soya sauce, ½ tsp salt
pinch of ajinomoto, optional

1. Soak the bread slice in water for a second. Squeeze out the water and crumble into a large bowl. Add cauliflower, plain flour, cornflour, rice flour if available, chilli powder, pepper, baking soda and salt into the bowl and mix well. Sprinkle 1-2 tsp water if needed to form balls.

2. Make oval balls of about 1" length. You will need to press the balls well with the fingers so that they bind properly.

3. Heat oil for frying. Fry 2-3 pieces at a time on medium or low heat till crisp and deep brown. Drain on paper napkins.

4. For the kothey sauce, heat oil in a pan. Reduce heat and add garlic. Stir. Add onion and capsicum and saute for 1 minute. Add hot and sweet sauce, soya sauce, salt, ajinomoto. Add ¼ cup water. Mix well. Remove from heat.

5. At the time of serving, heat the sauce, mix the kothey with the sauce and serve immediately.

MOONG DAL KI GOLI

Split green lentils are ground to a paste, cooked and made into small balls.

Serves 6-8

1 cup split green lentils (*dhuli moong dal*) - soaked for 2 hours
¼ tsp baking soda (*mitha soda*)
2-3 flakes garlic - chopped, 1 tbsp chopped ginger, 2 green chillies - chopped
4 tbsp oil
2 tbsp whole wheat flour (*atta*), a pinch asafoetida (*hing*)
¼ tsp turmeric (*haldi*), ½ tsp salt

COATING MASALA

2 tbsp oil
2 onions - chopped finely, 2 tomatoes - chopped finely
3-4 flakes garlic and ½" piece ginger - chopped finely
2 green chillies - deseeded and chopped
¼ tsp garam masala powder
¾ tsp salt
2 tsp tomato ketchup
2 tbsp chopped coriander

1. Drain dal. Grind dal with soda, garlic, ginger and green chillies to a paste. Grind the dal till you get a very soft and smooth paste.

2. Heat oil in a *kadhai*, add whole wheat flour and stir for a minute. Add asafoetida, turmeric, salt and dal paste. Cook on medium heat for about 4-5 minutes, stirring constantly till the mixture becomes thick and collects like a ball.

3. Remove from heat and while still warm shape the mixture into small marble sized balls. Keep aside.

4. For coating masala, heat oil in a *kadhai*, add the onions and cook till golden. Add ginger, garlic and green chillies. Cook till masala turns brown. Add tomatoes. Stir to mix well. Add salt, garam masala. Add ¼ cup water. Cook covered for 3-4 minutes on low heat. Add coriander and tomato ketchup. Keep aside.

5. At serving time, heat the masala and add moong ki golis, mix well and serve hot.

KATHI ROLLS

Wraps of soya granules flavoured with fresh coriander and mint.

Makes 8-10

8-10 roomali rotis or thin home made large rotis (wrap rotis in aluminium foil and put in a casserole)

1 cup thin sticks of cucumber (*kheera*) and 1 cup carrot sticks - to pickle

½ cup water, ½ cup white vinegar, ½ tsp salt, ½ tsp sugar

FILLING

1 cup nutri nuggets granules - soaked in 2 cups hot water for ½ hour

2 tbsp oil, ½ tsp cumin seeds (*jeera*), ¼ tsp nigella seeds (*kalonji*)

2 green chillies - chopped

4 onions - each cut into half and then widthwise to get half rings

½ tsp turmeric (*haldi*) powder, ½ tsp dry mango powder (*amchoor*)

3 tbsp tomato ketchup

¾ cup chopped coriander, 4 tbsp mint (*poodina*) - chopped roughly or torn with hands

2 capsicums - cut into 1" long, thin strips

1 tomato - deseeded & cut into 1" long, thin strips

1½ tsp salt, ¼ tsp pepper powder, ¾ tsp garam masala, ½ tsp red chilli powder

1. For the pickled veggies, mix water, vinegar, salt and sugar in a deep pan. Bring to a boil. Take the pan off the fire and add carrots and cucumber. Keep in the vinegar to cool.

2. For making the filling of kathi rolls, heat 1 tbsp oil in a pan, add cumin seeds and nigella seeds. Wait till cumin seeds turns golden. Add green chillies, fry for ½ minute on medium flame (do not brown them), add onions and stir till transparent on low heat for 5-7 minutes. Add nuggets, ½ tsp turmeric powder and dry mango powder. Stir on low heat for 5 minutes. Add ketchup, coriander and mint. Mix for 1-2 minutes.

3. Add capsicum and cook for a minute. Add salt, pepper powder, garam masala and red chilli powder. Cook for 2-3 minutes. Lastly add the tomato fingers and mix lightly. Remove from fire.

4. To assemble the kathi roll, take one roomali roti. Place some filling in the centre. Put some pickled veggies on it. Fold the sides to get a roll. Heat 1 tbsp oil in a pan and warm the roll by putting the joint side down in oil first. Turn carefully with a flat spoon when light golden from the bottom. Pan fry for a minute. Serve with hari chutney and some pickled veggies.

MEXICAN TOASTADAS

An excellent party snack!

Serves 10-12

1 tin baked beans, 1 tbsp butter, a bottle of tomato salsa
6 flour tortillas (buy ready-made or see recipe given below)

SALAD FILLING

1 onion - finely chopped, ½ cup corn, 1 tomato - deseeded and chopped
1 cup shredded ice berg lettuce, use cabbage if ice berg lettuce is unavailable
1 tbsp thick salsa, salt and pepper to taste

SOUR CREAM

1 cup yogurt (curd) - hang for 30 minutes in a muslin cloth
2 tbsp cream, ¼ tsp salt, 1 tsp lemon juice

1. Cut the tortillas with a cookie cutter or a sharp edged lid into small rounds of about 2" diameter. Prick with a fork. Deep fry 2-3 at a time on low medium heat till crisp & light golden. Let them cool completely. Store in an air tight jar.

2. Cook 1 cup baked beans with 1 tbsp butter till dry. Add a pinch of salt. Mash lightly to get a paste.

3. Mix all ingredients of the sour cream and refrigerate.

4. Mix all ingredients of the filling and check salt and pepper.

5. To serve, spread 1 tbsp of bean mixture at room temperature on a fried toastada. Put salad on it. Put a tsp of salsa and top with ½ tsp sour cream. Serve.

FLOUR TORTILLAS & TOASTADAS

Makes 6-7

1½ cups plain flour (*maida*), ½ tsp salt, 2 tbsp oil
¼ cup, approx. warm water to make the dough

1. Mix plain flour with oil and salt. Knead with enough warm water to get a firm and smooth dough. Knead further till dough is elastic and very smooth. Cover and keep aside for 30 minutes.

2. Roll out thin rotis or tortillas. Cut with a round lid or a cookie cutter to get toastadas. Prick with a fork. Deep fry 2-3 at a time on low medium heat till crisp and light golden. Let them cool completely. Store in an air tight jar.

MUSHROOM SHOOTERS

Makes 6-7

200 gm (10-12) small mushrooms - remove the stalk carefully and keep whole
¼ of red or green capsicum - cut into ½" pieces (6-7 pieces)
a few medium wooden skewers

MARINADE
2 tbsp soya sauce
1 tsp grated ginger, 1 tsp crushed garlic
rind of 1 lemon, 1 tsp lemon juice
1 tsp brown sugar or gur, 1 tbsp oil
¼ tsp red chilli flakes, ¼ tsp salt, 1 tsp ground cumin (*jeera powder*)

1. Mix all ingredients of the marinade together in a bowl.

2. Trim the stalks. Add mushroom caps, stalks and capsicum to the marinade &
   leave aside for at least one hour in the marinade. You can leave longer if you like.

3. At serving time, on a wooden stick, thread a mushroom cap side ways, keeping
   it flat, then a stalk, again a mushroom and a stalk. Finally top with a small
   piece of capsicum.

4. Heat 1-2 tbsp oil in a large non stick pan to grease the bottom of the pan. Put the
   skewers on it. Press lightly. Reduce heat. When the underside turns brown after 2-
   3 minutes, turn the side. Brown the other side also on low heat for 2-3 minutes.
   Spoon any left over marinade on the skewers. Remove from pan and serve hot.

FETA BRUSCHETTA WITH ROASTED PEPPERS

Serves 6-8

1 french loaf

4 tbsp (50 gm) butter, 2 cloves garlic - crushed, 1 tsp oregano

TOPPING

1 large red capsicum (red bell pepper) - roasted

½ cup sliced black olives, 200 gm paneer - cut into ¼" cubes

1 large spring onion - finely chopped with greens

2-3 tbsp olive oil, 1 tsp oregano, 1 tsp chilli flakes, ¾ tsp salt, or to taste

½ cup finely grated parmesan or cheddar cheese

1. Melt butter, add garlic and oregano. Cut french loaf into ½" thick slices. Brush garlic butter on both sides of each slice. Grill on both sides until lightly toasted.

2. Prick the capsicum with a fork and hold it directly on a flame till blackened. Alternately, grill in an oven turning occasionally, until blackened on all sides. Cool, peel or rub off the charred skin, deseed and chop into small pieces.

3. Place roasted capsicum in a bowl, add olives, paneer, spring onions. Sprinkle oregano, olive oil, chilli flakes and salt. Mix well.

4. Top the toasted slices with the paneer mixture and sprinkle finely grated cheese on top. Serve as it or grill for 2-3 minutes till cheese melts. Serve immediately.

QUICK GARLIC BREAD

Prepare a good amount of garlic-butter spread and refrigerate.
Use instantly for a quick snack.

100 gms mozzarella cheese - grated

50 gms butter - softened, 1 tsp oregano

1 tsp red chilli flakes, 1 tbsp crushed garlic

1 french loaf - cut into slices and spread with butter

1. Place cheese in a big bowl. Add the butter and blend with an electric hand mixer till smooth. Add oregano, chilli flakes and garlic. Store this garlic butter-cheese spread in a container in the fridge.

2. At the time of serving, cut the french loaf diagonally into ½" thick pieces. Apply butter on one side. Grill for 5-6 minutes with butter side up, till crisp.

SMOKED MUSHROOM GALOUTI KEBABS

Enjoy the smoky flavour to the hilt! Too good to be true.

Makes 8

200 gm mushrooms, juice of 1 lemon
1 medium potato - boiled mashed
75 gms paneer - grated
4 tbsp ghee/oil
1 onion - chopped finely
1 tbsp finely chopped ginger, 2 green chillies - chopped finely
½ tsp turmeric (*haldi*), ½ tsp red chilli powder
1 tbsp chopped coriander leaves
½ tsp salt, or to taste, ½ tsp garam masala

SMOKING
2" piece for charcoal (take a piece from ironing man)

GARNISH
lemon slices, onion rings, mint leaves, chaat masala to sprinkle

1. Boil 3 cups water with 1 tsp salt and juice of lemon. Add mushrooms and boil for 3-4 minutes. Strain. Chop finely. Keep aside.

2. Heat ghee or oil in a *kadhai*, add onions and saute till brown. Add ginger and green chillies, turmeric and chilli powder. Stir for a few seconds. Add the mushrooms, mashed potatoes and paneer. Mix well and remove from heat.

3. Add green coriander, salt and garam masala. Mash well with a potato masher or a *kadchhi*.

4. Place the mixture in a bowl. Place a small steel vessel (*katori*) in the center of the bowl. Hold the charcoal with a long tongs (*chimta*) and place it on fire. When it starts burning, place the live charcoal in the katori, pour 1 tsp ghee on the charcoal and immediately cover the bowl. Leave to smoke the mixture for 5 minutes.

5. Make kebabs of the smoked mixture.

6. Heat a non stick pan or a *tawa*, grease with ½ tsp oil. Shape the mixture into flattened roundels (*kebabs*) and cook on medium heat till brown. Garnish with lemon slices, onion rings, mint leaves and sprinkle chat masala.

CHATPATA HARYALI PANEER

Cottage cheese flavoured with a fragrant green paste.

Makes 12-15 pieces

300 gms paneer
2-3 tbsp oil
4 tbsp gram flour (*besan*), 1 tbsp oil
2 cubes cheddar cheese - finely grated (8 tbsp)

GREEN PASTE (*HARYALI PASTE*)
½ cup green coriander
½ raw mango - grated (¼ cup)
3 green chillies
1 tbsp chopped ginger
½ tsp cumin seeds (*jeera*), 3-4 cloves (*laung*)
3-4 pepper corns (*saboot kali mirchi*)
1 tsp ground cinnamon (*dalchini* powder)
½ tsp rock salt (*kala namak*)
1 tsp chaat masala

GARNISH
2 onions - cut into rings, a few mint leaves

1. Cut paneer into slightly thick (½" thick) triangular pieces. Cut a slit from one tip almost till the end, but keep the piece whole.

2. Heat 1 tbsp oil in a non stick pan. Add gram flour and roast for 2 minutes on low heat till fragrant.

3. Grind all the ingredients of the green paste to a thick paste. Remove to a flat bowl. Fill some paste in the slit of the paneer triangles.

4. To the remaining paste, add roasted gram flour and grated cheese. Check salt.

5. Marinate paneer in the prepared paste for 10-15 minutes.

6. At the time of serving, heat 2 tbsp oil in a non stick pan, roll the pan to spread the oil evenly in the pan. Place 4-5 pieces of paneer and shallow fry on medium heat till the paste sticks to the paneer.

7. Place on a serving dish. Saute onions rings in 1 tbsp oil till golden. Add mint leaves. Sprinkle chaat masala and remove from fire. Garnish paneer with golden onion rings and mint leaves. Serve hot.

VEGETABLE SHIKAMPURI KEBAB

Makes 12

1 cup chopped carrots - boiled
½ cup chopped beans - boiled
½ cup chopped cauliflower - boiled
4 potatoes - boiled and grated
4 tsp oil
2 green chillies - chopped finely
1 tsp finely chopped ginger
½ tsp turmeric (*haldi*), 2 tsp chilli powder
1 tbsp chopped coriander, 1 tbsp chopped mint
salt to taste
2 fresh bread slices - grind in a mixer to get fresh bread crumbs

FLAVOURING POWDER (CRUSH TOGETHER)
1 tsp cumin seeds (*jeera*), 4 green cardamoms (*chhoti illaichi*)
2-3 pepper corns (*saboot kali mirch*), 2-3 cloves (*laung*)
2 blades mace (*javitri*) and ½ tsp carom seeds (*ajwain*)

FILLING
¼ cup grated paneer, ¼ cup yogurt - hang for 20 minutes in a muslin cloth
1 onion - chopped
¼ cup khoya mashed
1 tbsp chopped mint
¼ tsp salt, or to taste

1. Heat oil in a *kadhai*, add ginger and green chillies. Let ginger turn golden.

2. Add carrots, beans, cauliflower. Stir fry for 2 minutes. Add turmeric and chilli powder. Stir for a few seconds.

3. Add grated potatoes and mix well.

4. Add salt, coriander and mint leaves. Add flavouring powder. Cook for about 5 minutes till the mixture is well blended. Remove from heat.

5. Add enough bread crumbs to make firm round balls. Check salt and spices.

6. For the filling, brown the chopped onions in 1 tbsp oil on low heat. Remove from heat and let it cool. Add all other ingredients of the filling and mix well.

7. Flatten balls, stuff filling and shape into kebabs. Keep in the fridge for sometime to set well. Shallow fry in a pan in 2-3 tbsp oil till crisp and golden brown. Sprinkle some chaat masala on the hot kebabs and serve.

FLAMING BABY CORNS

Serves 6-8

MARINATE TOGETHER
200 gms small baby corns
1 tomato - deseeded and cut into triangles
1 capsicum - cut into triangles
1 tsp garlic crushed
½ tsp salt and ¼ tsp pepper
2 tsp soya sauce

BATTER
¼ cup rice flour, ¼ cup cornflour
½ tsp salt, ¼ tsp pepper

OTHER INGREDIENTS
2 tbsp oil
1 tsp crushed garlic
2 tbsp finely chopped celery or onion
1-2 green chillies - deseeded and chopped
1 tbsp vinegar, 1 tbsp chilli sauce (red)
1 tsp soya sauce, 4 tbsp tomato ketchup
½ tsp salt and ¼ tsp pepper

1. Marinate babycorns, tomato and capsicum with garlic, soya sauce, salt and pepper for at least 1 hour or even more.

2. Mix all ingredients of a batter, adding enough water gradually to get a coating batter of a pouring consistency.

3. To deep fry, heat 1/3 of a *kadhai* with oil (1½ cups oil). Do not fill too much oil in the *kadhai*. Dip babycorns in batter and fry 10-12 pieces at a time on low medium heat till golden brown and crisp. Keep aside. Do not fry tomatoes and capsicums.

4. Heat 2 tbsp oil. Reduce heat. Add garlic. Stir. Add finely chopped celery or onion and 1-2 deseeded and chopped green chillies. Stir for a minute.

5. Remove from fire. Add vinegar, soya sauce, tomato sauce and chilli sauce, salt and pepper. Return to fire and cook the sauces on low heat for 1 minute. Keep aside till serving time.

6. To serve, refry babycorns in hot oil till crisp. Add to the prepared sauces and mix. Add capsicums and tomatoes. Stir for 1-2 minutes. If you like, add 1 tbsp red chilli sauce on the vegetables and mix well. Remove from fire. Serve.

SPICY POTATO BATONS

Beautiful to look at and delicious to eat!

Serves 4

2 large potatoes (or 200 gm paneer may be used)
1 tbsp grated or very finely chopped garlic, 1 tbsp lemon juice, 2 tbsp oil, ½-¾ tsp salt
1 tbsp very finely grated cheddar and 1 tbsp very finely grated mozzarella cheese

DRY ROAST TOGETHER

4 dry red chillies, 1 tsp coriander seeds (*saboot dhania*), ½ tsp cumin seeds
4 black pepper corns, 2" piece cinnamon, 4 cloves (*laung*), ¼ tsp nutmeg (*jaiphal*) pd.

1. Cut potatoes into ¼" thick slices. Cut slices into ¼" broad fingers or batons. Boil potatoes in 4 cups water with 1 tsp salt and 1 tbsp lemon juice for 4-5 minutes till crisp tender. Strain and pat dry on a clean kitchen towel.

2. Dry roast all ingredients on a *tawa* for 2-3 minutes. Place the roasted spices with garlic, oil and lemon juice in a grinder and grind to a coarse paste. Remove to a flat dish. Add salt & marinate the potato fingers in the paste till serving time.

3. To serve, cover a grill rack with aluminium foil. Grease it with some oil. Place fingers on it. Sprinkle both cheeses on them. Grill the potatoes for about 10- 12 minutes or till they turn golden. Serve hot. If using paneer, grill for just 4-5 minutes.

NUTTY LOTUS STEM BITES

Serves 6

100 gms (1 small) lotus stem (*kamal kakri/bhein*) - peeled, sliced into thin diagonal pieces and boiled in salted water for 7-8 minutes or till soft

PEANUT COATING

½ cup roasted peanuts, ½ cup coconut milk, 2 tbsp shredded fresh basil or coriander
¾ tsp salt, ½ tsp red chilli flakes, rind of 1 lemon, 2 tsp brown sugar or *gur*
1 tsp soya sauce, ½" piece of ginger - grated (1 tsp), 2 tsp lemon juice
1 tsp garlic paste, ¾ tsp cumin (*jeera*) powder, ½ tsp coriander (*dhania*) powder

1. Grind peanuts to a paste with coconut milk. Mix all the other ingredients of the peanut coating with the peanut paste in a bowl. Pat dry the boiled lotus stem and mix nicely with the marinade. Keep aside till serving time.

2. Heat 2 tbsp oil in a pan to grease the bottom of the pan. Reduce heat. Put the lotus stem pieces on it. Cook for 2 minutes. Do not turn till you get a golden brown colour on the underside. Turn and brown the other side also. Serve hot.

Steaming Soups

EMERALD SOUP

Serves 4

2 cups spinach (*paalak*) - chopped roughly
1 cup peas, 1 onion - chopped, 1 potato - chopped
2 green chillies - chopped, 4 large garlic cloves (2 tbsp), 2 tsp chopped ginger
4 cloves (*laung*), 1 bay leaf (*tej patta*)
2 tbsp butter
1 tsp salt and ½ tsp pepper, or to taste
½ cup milk, 50 gm paneer - cut into thin small pieces

1. Heat 2 tbsp butter in a pressure cooker, add onions and saute for 1 minute. Add spinach, peas, potato, green chillies, garlic, ginger, cloves and bay leaf. Saute for 1 minute. Add 4 cups of water and pressure cook to give 1 whistle. Remove from fire and let the pressure drop by itself. Cool the mixture.

2. Remove the bay leaf & blend the mixture in a liquidizer. Strain through a seive.

3. Heat the soup, add salt pepper and milk.

4. Add paneer and serve hot.

MUSHROOM AND VERMICELLI SOUP

A hearty soup!

Serves 4

200 gm mushrooms - chopped finely, 1 medium size onion - chopped finely
1½ tbsp butter, ¼ cup vermicelli (bambino), 1 bay leaf (*tej patta*)
2 tbsp finely chopped carrots, 2 tbsp finely chopped green capsicum
½ cup milk, 1 tsp salt and ½ tsp pepper, or to taste
2 tsp worcestershire sauce

1. Heat butter in a thick bottom sauce pan. Add onion and mushrooms. Saute over gentle or low flame for 2-3 minutes till onions get soft. Do not brown the onions.

2. Add 5 cups water and bring it to a boil. Add bay leaf and vermicelli, simmer for about 5-6 minutes till vermicelli is cooked.

3. Add carrot and capsicum. Add milk, salt and pepper and give one last boil. Remove from fire. Add worcestershire sauce. Mix. Serve hot.

TAMATAR & TULSI SHORBA

Serves 4-5

500 gms (6 medium) red tomatoes - chopped roughly, 2 onions - chopped
2 tsp chopped ginger, 2 tsp chopped garlic, 2 green chillies - deseed and chop
½ cup tulsi or basil, 8-10 curry leaves
1¼ tsp salt, ¼ tsp or less red chilli powder, ½ tsp sugar or to taste

WHOLE SPICES (COARSELY CRUSHED)

3 green cardamom, 3 cloves (*laung*), 1 black cardamom, 2 blades of mace (*javitri*)

TEMPERING

1 tbsp butter, ½ tsp garlic - finely sliced and chopped
2 tbsp shredded tulsi or basil, ½ tsp crushed cumin seeds (*jeera*)
¼ tsp pepper corns (*saboot kali mirch*) - crushed

1. Melt butter in a pressure cooker. Add coarsely crushed whole spices. Stir for 1-2 minutes. Put chopped garlic, ginger, onions, tomatoes, green chillies, tulsi, curry leaves, salt, red chilli powder, sugar and 5 cups water. Pressure cook to give 1 whistle. Remove from fire. When the pressure drops, strain. Do not grind in a mixer.

2. Put the strained soup again on fire. Boil. Simmer for 4-5 minutes on low flame.

3. For tempering, heat butter in a pan. Add garlic and fry till garlic changes colour. Put shredded tulsi and stir. Add crushed cumin. Saute for a minute. Remove from fire. Add crushed pepper and stir for a few seconds. Add this tempering to the soup. Serve hot.

LEMON - CORIANDER SOUP

Serves 4

1 tbsp oil, ½ tsp crushed garlic, 1 green chilli - deseeded and chopped
4 mushrooms - very thinly sliced (paper thin slices)
2" piece of carrot - very thinly sliced (you can get thin slices with a peeler)
2 tbsp tiny florets of cauliflower, 1 vegetable soup/stock cube, ¾ tsp pepper
1 tsp salt, or to taste, 2 tbsp cornflour mixed in ¼ cup water
1 cup fresh coriander with stems - grind roughly, 3-4 tbsp lemon juice

1. Heat oil in a deep pan, add garlic and green chilli. Saute for 1-2 minutes.

2. Add vegetables. Saute for 1 minute. Add 4 cups water. Add salt, pepper and stock cube.

3. Boil. Add the cornflour paste & bring to a boil again. Keep aside till serving time. To serve, boil soup. Add lemon juice and coriander. Serve hot.

CHILLED CURRIED APPLE & MINT SOUP

Serve soup cold. If you like it hot, serve with a swirl of cream instead of yogurt.

Serves 4

2 tbsp butter, 1 onion - roughly chopped, 1 tbsp curry powder (MDH)
4 cups vegetable stock, given below
2 apples - peeled, seeded and roughly chopped
1½ tbsp mango chutney, 3 tbsp lemon juice, or to taste
¼ cup finely chopped fresh mint
1½ tsp salt and ¾ tsp black pepper, or to taste, 100 gm (½ cup) plain yogurt

STOCK

6 cups water, 1 tsp pepper corns (*saboot kali mirch*), 2 bay leaves
1 carrot - roughly chopped, 1½ cups roughly chopped cabbage, 1 onion - chopped

1. For the stock, boil all ingredients of the stock together. Cover and simmer for 10 minutes to get about 4 cups of stock. Strain & discard vegetables & spices.

2. Melt the butter in a large saucepan, add the onion & cook gently, stirring occasionally, for a few minutes until soft but not coloured. Add the curry powder & cook, stirring constantly, for 1-2 minutes. Add 4 cups stock. If stock is less add enough water to make upto 4 cups. Add chopped apples & bring to a boil, stirring. Cover & simmer for 15 minutes or until the apples are tender.

3. Puree apples with mango chutney and lemon juice in a mixer until very smooth.

4. Add chopped mint, salt and pepper to taste. Serve hot with a swirl of cream. If you like it cold, cover and chill in the refrigerator for at least 3 hours. Whisk in the yogurt, then taste for seasoning. If the soup is too thick, add a little milk.

HOT & SOUR SOUP

Serves 4-5

CHILLI-GARLIC PASTE (1 tsp ready-made paste may be used)
2-3 dry red chillies - deseeded and soaked in water for 10 minutes
2 flakes garlic, 1 tsp vinegar
1 tsp oil

OTHER INGREDIENTS
2 tbsp oil
1-2 tender French beans - sliced very finely (3-4 tbsp)
1-2 tbsp dried mushrooms or 2-3 fresh mushrooms - chopped
½ cup chopped cabbage
½ cup thickly grated carrot
6 cups hot water
2 vegetable seasoning cubes (maggi) - crushed
2 tsp sugar
1¼ tsp salt
½ tsp pepper powder, or to taste
1- ½ tbsp soya sauce
2 tbsp vinegar
2 tbsp tomato ketchup
6-7 level tbsp cornflour mixed with ½ cup water

1. Soak dry, red chillies in a little water for 10 minutes.

2. For the chilli-garlic paste, drain the red chillies. Grind red chillies, garlic, vinegar and oil roughly with in a small coffee or spice grinder. You can use 1 tsp red chilli paste if you like.

3. If dried mushrooms are available, boil them in water for 5 minutes to soften. Wash thoroughly to clean the dirt in them. Cut away any hard portion and then cut into smaller pieces.

4. Heat 2 tbsp oil. Add chilli-garlic paste. Stir. Add beans and mushrooms. Stir fry for 1-2 minutes on high flame. Add cabbage and carrots. Stir for a few seconds.

5. Add the water and the seasoning cubes. Add sugar, salt, pepper, soya sauce, vinegar and ketchup. Boil for 2 minutes.

6. Add cornflour paste, stirring continuously. Cook for 2-3 minutes till the soup turns thick. Serve hot.

MINESTRONE

A hearty Italian soup. A few toasted slices will make a complete meal.

Serves 4-5

STOCK
7 cups water
1 cup cabbage - roughly chopped, 2 onions - roughly chopped
1 carrot - roughly chopped, 2 bay leaves (*tej patta*)

OTHER INGREDIENTS
2 tbsp olive oil or any cooking oil
1 onion - chopped finely, 3-4 tbsp finely chopped celery, 2 flakes garlic - crushed
1 small potato - diced into very small pieces (½ cup)
1 carrot - diced into small pieces, remove core (½ cup)
½ cup zucchini - diced into small pieces with skin
3 medium sized tomatoes - blanched, peeled and chopped finely
½ cup tomato puree
¾ tsp salt, pepper to taste, ½ tsp oregano
¼ cup of macaroni or any other small pasta - boiled (½ cup)
8-10 fresh basil leaves - torn into pieces or shredded

GARNISHING
2 tbsp finely grated cheddar cheese

1. For stock, mix all ingredients given under stock with 7 cups of water. Bring to a boil. Keep on low flame for 15 minutes. Strain the stock. Keep the liquid stock aside. Discard the solids.

2. To blanch the tomatoes, put them in boiling water for 3-4 minutes. Remove from water and peel them to remove skin. Chop them very finely. Keep aside.

3. Heat oil. Add onion, celery and garlic. Stir fry till onions turn golden brown.

4. Add potato, carrot and zucchini. Stir fry for 1-2 minutes.

5. Add tomatoes. Cook 2-3 minutes.

6. Add the prepared stock, about 5 cups. Give one boil. Lower heat. Add macaroni & tomato puree. Add salt, pepper and oregano to taste. Simmer for 5-7 minutes till macaroni is soft. Add basil. Serve hot, garnished with some grated cheese.

Note: Instead of fresh stock, 5 cups water and 2 seasoning cubes/soup cubes can be used. Do not add any salt, if using soup cubes as they already contain salt. Taste at the end and adjust salt to taste.

STIR FRIED SALAD

Serves 4

3 tbsp olive oil
2 thin, long brinjals - cut into 1" cubes without peeling
2 zucchinis - cut into 1" cubes without peeling
8-10 flakes garlic - sliced, 1 large onion - cut into 8 pieces and separated
1 capsicum - cut into 1" pieces, 1 cup cabbage - cut into 1" pieces
8-10 black olives - sliced, 3½ tbsp vinegar, 1 tsp oregano, ¾ tsp pepper, ¾ tsp salt

1. Heat 1 tbsp olive oil in a non stick pan and add the brinjals. Stir fry for 3-4 minutes till brown patches appear. Lower heat, cover and cook for 1 minute till the brinjal pieces are cooked but firm. Remove from pan to a bowl.

2. In the same pan heat 1 tbsp oil and add zucchini. Stir fry for 2-3 minutes. Reduce heat, cover and cook till slightly tender but firm. Remove to the bowl.

3. Heat 1 tbsp oil again in the pan. Add garlic, stir and add onion, capsicum and cabbage. Stir for 2 minutes till well coated in oil. Remove to the same bowl with brinjal and zucchini.

4. Add chopped olives to the stir fried vegetables.

5. In a cup, mix vinegar, salt, pepper and oregano. Pour over the stir fried salad and mix well. Cover with a wrap and chill. Serve cold or at room temperature.

PEANUT AND GRAPE SALAD

Serves 2-3

¾ cup peanuts, 1 tbsp butter, 1 tsp chopped garlic
1 spring onion - chopped along with the greens, ½ cup chopped grapes
½ cup finely chopped capsicum, ½ tomato - deseeded and finely chopped

DRESSING
2 tbsp olive oil, 1 tbsp mayonnaise, 2 tsp chat masala
1 tsp lemon juice, ¼ tsp salt and ¼ tsp pepper, 2 tbsp chopped mint

1. Heat 1 tbsp butter. Add garlic and stir. Add peanuts and stir for 5 minutes till golden. Add spring onions and stir. Keep aside till serving time.

2. Mix together grapes, capsicum & tomato. Mix all the ingredients of the dressing and mix with the grapes and vegetables. Refrigerate.

3. To serve, add the peanuts and the spring onions. Toss to mix well. Serve.

SPINACH ORANGE SALAD

Serves 4-6

200 gms spinach (firm & fresh bundle with small sized leaves), 2 big, firm oranges

DRESSING
4 tbsp olive oil, 2 tbsp honey
½ tsp light soya sauce, 2 tbsp white vinegar, ½ tsp salt

TOPPING
6-7 almonds, 1 tbsp sesame seeds (*til*)

1. Remove the stems of the spinach. Soak the spinach leaves for 15 minutes in a bowl of cold water to which ice cubes are added. Remove from water and pat dry on a kitchen towel. Tear into big pieces.

2. Remove fibres from each segment of orange. Slightly cut each orange segment from the joint end and remove the fibrous covering and the seeds. Keep aside.

3. Mix all the ingredients of the dressing in a small spice grinder or with a whisk till the dressing turns slightly thick.

4. Toast the almonds in a microwave for 2 minutes in a pan on low heat for 2-3 minutes till fragrant. Cut almonds into slices. Toast the sesame seed also in a pan till crisp and light golden. Keep nuts aside.

5. At the time of serving, pour the dressing over the spinach and orange segments, toss to mix well. Remove the salad into a shallow flat platter, top with toasted almonds and sesame seeds. Serve immediately.

BOMBAY SALAD

Alphanso mangoes, a specialty of Bombay are used in the salad.

Serves 4-6

2 cups boiled long grain basmati rice
1 cup ripe mango, preferably alphanso mangoes - finely chopped
½ cup capsicum - finely chopped, 1 tomato - deseeded and finely chopped
1 spring onion - finely chopped

DRESSING
4 tbsp oil, 2 tsp sugar
1 tbsp vinegar
½ tsp pepper powder, ¼ tsp mustard powder, ½ tsp salt

1. Pour all the ingredients of the dressing in a tight lid bottle & shake well till thick.

2. Mix all the other ingredients of the salad in a bowl. Pour dressing over the salad and mix well. Serve cold.

SPRING VEGETABLES AND PASTA SALAD

Serves 4

1½ cups farfalle (bow pasta), 1 tsp olive oil
½ cup tomato - chopped into ½" pieces, 1 small capsicum - chopped into ½" pieces
½ cup spring onions - chopped into ½" pieces
½ cup greens of spring onion chopped into ½" pieces

DRESSING
3 tbsp olive oil, 1½ tbsp brown vinegar
1½ tbsp crushed garlic
1 tbsp chilli sauce, ½ tsp chilli flakes, ½ tsp salt

1. Boil the pasta till soft but firm. Drain and refresh under cold water. Add 1 tsp olive oil and mix.

2. Mix all the ingredients for the dressing and whisk together till well blended.

3. In a large bowl put the pasta and the vegetables. Add the dressing. Toss together to mix well. Refrigerate till serving time.

FRUIT & VEGETABLE PASTA SALAD

Serves 6

½ cup bow pasta (farfalle), 1 tsp olive oil
¼ cup black grapes, ¼ cup green grapes
2-3 slices fresh or tinned pineapple - cut into small cubes
½ red apple - cut into small cubes with the peel
1 small cucumber - cut into thin slices without peeling
5-6 mint leaves
½ capsicum - cut into small cubes
1 cup thinly shredded lettuce

DRESSING

1 cup (250 gms) curd - hang for 15 minutes in a muslin cloth and squeeze lightly
1 tbsp olive oil
1 tbsp powdered sugar
½ tsp salt, ½ tsp pepper
¾ tsp mustard powder or to taste
2 tbsp cream, preferably thick (amul)
1 tbsp orange marmalade (optional)

GARNISH

2 tbsp walnuts - toasted

1. Boil pasta in 3 cups of water to which 1 tsp salt has been added. Cook till soft yet firm. Drain & refresh under cold water. Mix 1 tsp olive oil and keep aside.

2. Place all the ingredients of the salad, except pasta and tomatoes in a bowl of chilled water for ½ hour to make them crisp.

3. Mix all the ingredients of the dressing till smooth. Refrigerate till serving time.

4. Drain the fruit and vegetables from the chilled water and pat dry on the kitchen towel well. There should be no moisture in the salad as the salad dressing will become thin and not coat the fruits and vegetables nicely. Put the vegetables & pasta in a big mixing bowl. Wrap with a cling film. Refrigerate till serving time.

5. To serve, pour the dressing over the salad and toss to mix well. Garnish with toasted walnuts.

Tantalizing Taste of Raitas

MOOLI KA RAITA

Yogurt spiked with radish.

Serves 6

2 cups yogurt (curd)
½ tsp salt, 2 tsp sugar
1 green chilli - finely chopped
2 tbsp fresh tender leaves of radish (*mooli*)
1 cup radish (*mooli*) grated (loosely packed), do not squeeze it

TEMPERING

1½ tbsp oil
8-10 curry leaves
½ tsp nigella seeds (*kalonji*), ½ tsp cumin seeds (*jeera*)
¼ tsp red chilli powder

1. Beat the yogurt with salt and sugar. Add green chillies, radish and the leaves. Transfer to a serving bowl.

2. Heat oil in a small tempering pan, add curry leaves, cumin seeds and nigella seeds. Let cumin seeds turn golden. Add red chilli powder and remove from fire. Pour the tempering over the yogurt. Serve cold.

CREAMY PAPAYA RAITA

A party raita. Ice cream is the surprise ingredient which makes it so creamy.

Serves 6

1 cup finely chopped ripe papaya
2 cups fresh yogurt
6 tbsp vanilla ice cream
2 tbsp chopped mint, 2 tbsp finely chopped green coriander
½ tsp black salt, ½ tsp salt, ¼ tsp pepper, or to taste

GARNISH

a few papaya balls, mint sprig

1. Beat the yogurt with salt, black salt, pepper. Add ice cream and beat well till creamy. Add coriander and mint.

2. Mash papaya with a fork, add to the curd, mx well.

3. Turn into a serving bowl, garnish and serve cold.

NUTTY SPINACH RAITA

Serves 4-6

24 fresh spinach leaves
2 cups fresh yogurt/curd, ¼ tsp black salt, or to taste
2 tbsp peanuts, 12 almonds, 12 cashewnuts
1 tsp sesame seeds (*til*), 4 tbsp black raisins (*kaali kishmish*)

TEMPERING
1½ tbsp oil, ½ tsp mustard seeds (*rai*), 6-8 curry leaves

1. Pour ½ cup water in a *kadhai* or a sauce pan. Bring to a boil & add the spinach. Cook for ½ minute till the spinach wilts slightly but still retains its colour and shape. Drain and refresh under cold water. Squeeze out excess water and chop.

2. Heat a non stick pan and dry roast peanuts, almonds and cashewnuts till fragrant. Remove from pan and add sesame seeds to the pan. Roast till they change colour. Remove from pan and add raisins. Dry roast for 1-2 minutes till crisp. Keep aside.

3. Place the almonds, peanuts and cashewnuts in a dry blender and churn for a second to crush the nuts roughly. Keep aside.

4. Beat the yogurt with salt and black salt, add chopped spinach, toasted nuts, sesame seeds and raisins.

5. Transfer raita to a serving bowl. Heat oil in a tempering pan, add mustard seeds. Let them crackle. Add curry leaves, stir till transparent and immediately pour over the raita. Serve cold.

CREAMY STRAWBERRY RAITA

Serves 4-6

2 cups fresh yogurt
1 cup fresh strawberries - chopped
4-6 tbsp strawberry ice cream
salt to taste
2 tbsp chopped mint

1. Beat the yogurt, add salt, mint and ice cream. Mix well.

2. Transfer to a serving bowl and add finely chopped strawberries. Mix lightly. Serve.

Fusion Stir-Fries

Stir-fry is a quick and instant way of cooking. It is generally cook and serve. Cut all vegetables and keep in a plate covered with a plastic wrap till serving time. The sauces should be collected together in a small bowl before you start cooking. A wok or a large kadhai is the utensil used for stir -fries as the large surface area helps to evaporate the water quite fast, which in turn makes a good stir-fry. Cook on high flame, stirring constantly.

HERBED BEANS WITH POTATOES

Serves 4

250 gm french beans - cut into 2" long, pieces
2 medium potatoes - cut into thin long pieces, 2 tbsp butter, 1 tbsp oil
1 tsp onion seeds (*kalonji*), 2-3 dried red chillies - broken into pieces
6-8 flakes garlic - chopped (1 tbsp)
2 tbsp chopped fresh coriander, 2 tbsp chopped fresh mint
1 tsp sugar, preferably brown sugar, ¾ tsp salt, 1 tbsp lemon juice

1. Mix coriander, mint, sugar, salt and lemon juice together.

2. Heat butter and oil in a non stick *kadhai* or a wok. Reduce heat. Add onion seeds, red chillies and garlic. Stir for ½ minute on low heat.

3. Add the potatoes and stir for 2-3 minutes. Keep them spaced out while doing so. Cover and cook for about 5-7 minutes till crisp tender.

4. Add the french beans and ¼ tsp salt. Stir fry for 3-4 minutes on medium heat. Cover and cook for 2-3 minutes till soft but crunchy.

5. Remove from heat. Add the coriander-mint mixture and mix well. Serve hot with bread or as a side dish with an Indian meal.

STIR FRIED SCHEZWAN MUSHROOMS

Serves 4

200 gm mushrooms - each cut into half
2 cups spring onion chopped with the greens
2 tbsp oil, 2 tbsp chopped garlic

MIX TOGETHER IN A BOWL
4 tbsp schezwan sauce
2 tbsp tomato ketchup, 1 tsp honey (optional)
¼ tsp salt or to taste, 1 tsp All-in-one stir fry sauce, ¼ cup water

1. Heat oil in a non stick pan. Add garlic and stir for ½ minute. Add spring onions and cook for about 2 minutes till slightly soft.

2. Add the mushrooms and cook on medium heat for 2-3 minutes till golden.

3. Reduce heat. Pour the mixed sauces over the mushrooms and stir to coat mushrooms with the sauces. Remove from heat. Serve hot.

STIR FRIED GREENS IN BLACK BEAN SAUCE

Serves 6

2 bunches of bok choy - washed and stalks trimmed by just ½" from the bottom
100 gms snow peas or French beans - stringed
1 cup roughly chopped cabbage
2-3 tbsp olive oil
6-8 flakes garlic - sliced or chopped
4 tbsp black bean sauce, 2 tbsp tomato ketchup
1 tbsp cornflour
½ tsp roughly crushed black pepper, ¼ tsp salt

1. Boil 4 cups of water with 1 tsp salt and 1 tsp sugar in a pan. Add snowpeas or french beans. Remove from fire. Let them be in hot water for 2-3 minutes. Strain and refresh under cold water to retain the green colour. If using beans, cut them into long pieces diagonally. Keep aside.

2. Mix black bean sauce, ketchup, cornflour and ½ cup water in a bowl. Keep aside.

3. Heat olive oil in a non stick *kadhai* or a wok. Add garlic and stir. Add the cabbage. Stir for a minute. Add bokchoy and stir fry for 2-3 minutes. Add the blanched snow peas or french beans, stir for a minute.

4. Pour the mixed sauces and stir to coat the vegetables. Add salt and pepper. Serve hot.

OKRA STIR FRY

Serves 3-4

1 tbsp softened butter

200 gms okra (*bhindi*) - cut into half lengthwise

1 spring onion - chopped with greens

½ cup frozen green peas

½ yellow bell pepper (capsicum) - cut into 1" long diamond shapes

½ red bell pepper - cut into 1" long diamond shapes

STIR FRY SAUCE (MIX TOGETHER IN A CUP)

3 tbsp "all in one stir–fry sauce" (chings)

1 tsp vinegar, ½ cup water, 1 tbsp cornflour

½ tsp pepper, ½ tsp salt

1. Deep fry okra in 2-3 batches on high flame for 3-4 minutes till soft. Frying on low heat makes it chewy. Keep aside. Add only at serving time. Mix all ingredients of the sauce in a cup and keep aside. Cut vegetables and keep aside.

2. At serving time, heat butter in a non stick pan or wok. Add spring onions and stir for about 2 minutes till slightly soft. Add peas and stir for ½ minute.

3. Add yellow and red bell peppers. Cook for 2-3 minutes. Add the mixed sauces. Simmer for a minute.

4. Add fried okra and mix well. Serve hot with rice or noodles.

SUBZI STIR FRY

The Indian stir fry.

Serves 4

MIX TOGETHER
4 tbsp yogurt
2 tbsp tomato puree
1 tsp coriander (*dhania*) powder, ¼ tsp garam masala powder, ½ tsp chilli powder
½ tsp coarsely crushed pepper, ¾ tsp salt
seeds of 3 green cardamoms (*chhoti illaichi*) - crushed

OTHER INGREDIENTS
1 medium potato - cut into 8 pieces
1 carrot - cut into thin round slices
8-10 French beans - cut into 2" pieces
8-10 pieces cauliflower - cut into medium florets
1 tbsp butter, 1 tsp oil
1 bay leaf (*tej patta*)
1" piece cinnamon (*dalchini*)
1 onion - chopped
1 tsp chopped garlic, 1 tsp chopped ginger
2 green chillies - chopped

1. Boil 4 cups of water. Add 1 tsp of salt. Add potato. Boil for about 10 minutes till tender. Check with a knife. When the potatoes are done, remove from water. Add carrot, beans and cauliflower to the boiling water. Boil for 1 minute. Leave in hot water for 2 minutes till the vegetables turn crisp-tender. Strain and keep aside.

2. Mix together in a cup - curd, tomato puree, coriander powder, garam masala, chilli powder, pepper powder, salt and cardamon seeds. Keep aside.

3. Heat butter and oil in a *kadhai*, add bay leaf and cinnamon. Stir and add onions. Cook till light pink and add garlic, ginger and green chillies. Cook for ½ minute.

4. Reduce heat. Add the yogurt mixed with spices and stir fry for 1 minute till slightly thick.

5. Add the vegetables, stir on low flame to coat the masala on the vegetables. Mix well, serve hot with toasts or chappati.

Continental Cuisine

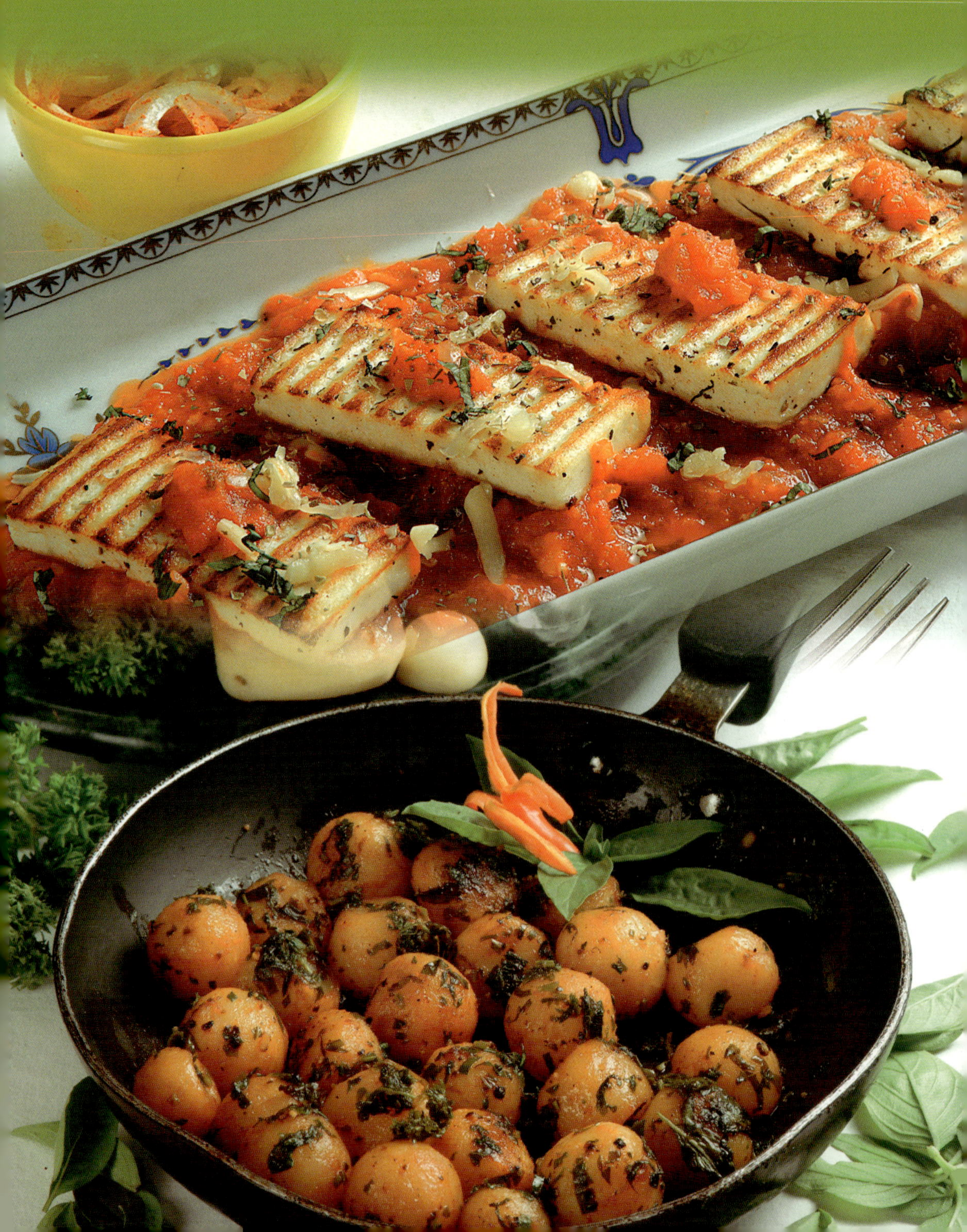

COTTAGE CHEESE STEAKS

Serves 4

COTTAGE CHEESE STEAKS

200 gms paneer - cut into 2" squares or rectangles of ½" thickness
½ tsp salt, ¼ tsp pepper, 1 tsp olive oil
2 tbsp chopped fresh basil leaves or fresh coriander

SAUCE

1 tbsp olive oil
500 gm (6) tomatoes - blanched, peeled and pureed
1 tsp chopped garlic, 1 small onion - chopped finely
1 tsp sugar, ½ tsp chilli flakes, 1 tsp salt
2 tbsp chopped fresh basil or coriander leaves

TOPPING (MIX TOGETHER)

50 gm (4 tbsp) parmesan cheese or cheddar cheese
1 tbsp fresh basil or any other herb, 1 tbsp olive oil

1. For steaks, marinate paneer slices with salt, pepper, olive oil & basil or coriander.

2. Boil tomatoes in water for 4 minutes. Remove skin and cool. Blend to a puree.

3. Heat oil in a pan, add garlic and onion. Saute till soft, add the tomato puree, salt, sugar and chilli flakes. Simmer on low heat for 10 minutes till a slightly thick sauce is ready.

4. Pan fry the marinated paneer slices on a grill pan or a non stick pan till golden brown marks appear. Do not over cook and harden the paneer. Heat the sauce. Place most of the tomato sauce in an oven proof flat dish or platter. Arrange steaks. Sprinkle the remaining sauce on the steaks. Sprinkle topping mixture.

5. To serve, grill in a preheated oven for 2-3 minutes till heated through or microwave for 1 minute. Serve with grilled french loaf.

SPRING ONION FLAN

Serves 8

TART
150 gms plain flour (*maida*)
75 gms salted butter - cut into cubes and chilled
2 tbsp cold water
pinch of salt

FILLING
1 tbsp butter or olive oil
9-10 large spring onions - chopped with the greens
2 tbsp cheese spread
2 tbsp thick cream/*malai*
¼ tsp oregano, ¼ tsp chilli flakes, ¼ tsp pepper, ¼ tsp salt, or to taste

TOPPING
1 firm tomato - cut into very thin slices
75 gms mozzarella cheese grated (¾ cup)
3 cubes cheddar cheese - grated (¾ cup)

1. Place plain flour in a bowl. Add salt and butter. Mix the butter into the flour with finger tips till it resembles bread crumbs.

2. Add water and gather into a firm dough. Do not knead too much. Keep aside covered in the fridge for 10-15 minutes. Remove from fridge and sprinkle dry flour on a rolling board. Roll the dough into a thin chappati between 2 sheets of polythene. Place it in the tart tin covering the sides too. Prick the tart and bake at 200°C/400°F in a preheated oven for 12-15 minutes till light golden.

3. For the filling, heat butter in a non stick pan and add the chopped spring onions. Cook till soft and water evaporates. Remove from heat. Add cheese spread, cream, oregano, chilli flakes, pepper and salt. Cool slightly.

4. To assemble, mix both cheeses together. Arrange the filling in the tart. Arrange the tomatoes, sprinkle the cheese over the filling and bake again at 200°C/400°F in a preheated oven for 15 minutes till the edges turn brown. Serve hot.

QUICK FUSILLI ALFREDO

Serves 2-3

2 cups fusilli pasta (spiral)
1 tbsp butter
3 spring onions - chopped diagonally, keeps greens separate
1½ tsp cornflour dissolved in ½ cup milk
¼ cup cream (optional)
¼ cup grated cheddar cheese
½ tsp salt, ¼ tsp pepper

1. Boil the pasta according to the instructions on the packet. Drain. Refresh under cold water. Keep aside.

2. Heat butter in a non stick pan, add the white of spring onions and saute for a minute.

3. Mix milk and cornflour. Add to the spring onions in the pan. Mix well.

4. Add cream and cheese, mix well. Keep alfredo sauce aside.

5. To serve, toss the pasta in the alfredo sauce. Add greens of spring onions. Sprinkle salt and pepper and mix till the sauce coats the pasta. Serve immediately.

VEGETABLE STEW

Serves 4

½ cup broccoli florets, ½ cup cauliflower florets
1 large carrot - cut into diagonal slices
4-5 French beans - cut into 2" pieces

BROWN SAUCE
2 tbsp butter, 2-3 flakes garlic
2½ tbsp plain flour (*maida*)
2 magic maggi cubes (veg stock cubes)
1 tsp worcestershire sauce, 1 tsp HP sauce, ½ tsp pepper

TOPPING
few blanched almonds, parsley, rind of 1 lemon

1. For the brown sauce, heat butter in a non stick pan, add garlic on low flame. Stir and add the plain flour and cook till slightly brown. Reduce heat and add 3 cups of water, bring to a boil. Add stock cubes, sauces and pepper.

2. Add the vegetables. Simmer for 3-4 minutes till the vegetables are slightly cooked. Transfer to a serving dish. Add the lemon rind, blanched almonds and parsley. Serve hot with steamed rice.

STUFFED MUSHROOM BAKE

Serves 4

200 gms mushrooms, preferably large size
a few whole pepper corns (*saboot kali mirch*)

FILLING

stalks of mushrooms - chopped finely
1 tbsp butter, 2 flakes garlic - crushed
2 tbsp finely chopped onion
4-5 basil leaves or ½ tsp oregano
¼ tsp pepper powder, ¼ tsp salt, or to taste
2 tbsp grated cheddar cheese

SAUCE

½ cup (100 gms) Amul cream, 1 tsp butter
½ tsp chilli flakes, ½ tsp dried oregano, ¼ tsp salt or to taste
2-3 tbsp milk

TOPPING (MIX TOGETHER)

4 tbsp fresh bread crumbs (1 slice bread - grind in a mixer)
1 tsp butter, 2 tbsp grated cheddar cheese, a pinch of pepper

1. Pull out the stalk or stem of the mushrooms. With the back of a spoon, gently scrape the inside of the mushrooms to get a hollow. Reserve the stalks for the filling.

2. Boil 2 cups water with 1 tsp lemon juice and ½ tsp salt. Add the mushrooms and blanch for 1 minute. Drain well.

3. For the filling, chop the stalks finely. Heat butter in a non stick pan and add garlic. Stir and add the onions. Saute for ½ minute and add the stalks. Stir till dry, add salt, pepper and basil leaves. Remove from heat and add the cheese. Mix well. Fill the mushroom hollow with the filling and keep aside.

4. For the sauce, pour cream in a small bowl, add butter, chilli flakes, oregano, salt and milk. Mix well and transfer most of it to a low sided (shallow), small baking dish, keeping some to top the mushrooms. Arrange the stuffed mushrooms on sauce.

5. Sprinkle topping mixture on the sauce and on the mushrooms. Dot mushrooms with the remaining sauce. Arrange a pepper corn on each mushroom. Grill for 10 minutes or bake at 200°C in a preheated oven for 10 minutes. Serve hot with garlic bread.

GRILLED VEGETABLE PLATTER

Serves 4

2 carrots - cut into thin, long fingers (2½" long)
6 asparagus spears - each cut into half
100 gms babycorns
1 thick zucchini - cut into slices diagonally
2 tomatoes - each cut into 8 wedges, pulp removed
1 long brinjal or aubergine - cut into 2" cubes
2 tbsp olive oil, ¾ tsp salt and ½ tsp pepper, or to taste

OTHER INGREDIENTS
2 tbsp olive oil
1 tbsp crushed chopped garlic
½ tbsp pepper corn (*saboot kali mirch*) crushed roughly
8-10 basil leaves
½ tsp oregano
2-3 tbsp balsamic vinegar or malt vinegar
4 tbsp grated parmesan or cheddar cheese, a sprig of basil

1. Boil 3 cups water with 1 tsp salt, 1 tsp lemon juice and 1 tsp sugar. Add carrots, asparagus and babycorns. Boil for about ½ minute and remove from fire. Let vegetables be in hot water for 2-3 minutes till crisp tender. Refresh veggies with ice cold water and drain veggies. Pat dry on a kitchen towel. Keep aside.

2. Make the marinade in a bowl with 2 tbsp olive oil and ¾ tsp salt and ½ tsp pepper. Put brinjals, tomatoes and zucchini in the marinade and mix very well. Add the blanched veggies also and mix. Grill all the vegetables in the oven or in a pan on fire.

3. Heat 2 tbsp olive oil in a wok, add garlic on low heat, stir and add pepper and oregano. Add the grilled vegetables and fresh basil. Cook on high heat, check the seasoning. Take off the heat, add balsamic vinegar and toss. Arrange on a platter. Top with cheese and a basil sprig. Serve immediately.

SIZZLER WITH GINGER ORANGE SAUCE

Serves 2

VEGETABLES
½" thick, diagonally cut slices of a thick zucchini (4-6 slices)
½" thick, diagonally cut slices of a thick long brinjal (4-6 slices)
¼" thick, diagonally cut slices of a thick carrot (4-6 slices)
4-6 mushrooms, 3-4 garlic flakes

MARINADE
3 tbsp olive oil, 1½ tbsp balsamic vinegar, 1 tsp rosemary, ¾ tsp salt, ¾ tsp pepper
1 tsp garlic paste, 1 tsp mustard paste

TO SERVE
3 cups boiled rice mixed with ½ tsp oregano, ½ tsp red chilli flakes, salt to taste
2 tbsp finely chopped coriander, 2 cabbage leaves - torn into pieces
3 tbsp oil mixed with 3 tbsp water & refrigerated

GINGER ORANGE SAUCE
2 tbsp olive oil
1 tsp lemon rind
1 tsp ginger juice (finely grate 1 tbsp ginger and squeeze)
1 cup water, 1 stock cube - crushed
¼ tsp salt, ¼ tsp pepper
4 tbsp Orange Tang and 3 tbsp cornflour dissolved in ¼ cup water
½ tbsp lemon juice, 2 tbsp shredded basil

1. Mix all ingredients of the marinade. Add vegetables to it. Keep aside for 30 minutes.

2. Mix rice with chopped coriander, salt, red chilli flakes and oregano to taste.

3. To prepare the sauce, heat 2 tbsp olive oil. Add water. Bring to a boil. Add stock cube, salt and pepper. Simmer on low heat for 2 minutes. Add tang and cornflour dissolved in water, stirring constantly. Cook for a minute. Remove from fire. Add lemon rind, ginger juice, lemon juice and basil.

4. To serve, heat a nonstick pan. Add the marinated veggies and without stirring much, pan fry vegetables till cooked and dry.

5. Heat the iron sizzler plate. Place a few cabbage leaves. Spread rice on the iron plate. Arrange the panfried veggies on the rice. Spoon sauce on the veggies. Spoon some cold mixture of oil and water on the wooden plate and place iron plate on it to sizzle and make fumes. Spoon some oil and water on the iron plate too. Serve hot.

VEGETABLE LASAGNA

Serves 6-8

6 lasagna sheets

1 cup grated cheddar cheese, 1 cup grated mozzarella cheese

RED VEGETABLE SAUCE

4 tbsp olive oil, 4 large tomatoes

8-10 flakes garlic - crushed, 1 onion - chopped, 1 small carrot - cut into small pieces

1 long brinjal (*baigan*) - peeled cut into small pieces

2 small zucchinis - cut into small pieces, ¼ cup corn kernels , ¼ cup peas

¼ cup tomato puree, 1 tbsp hot and sweet chilli sauce or tomato ketchup

1 tsp salt, 1 tsp oregano, 1 tsp red chilli flakes, a few basil leaves (optional)

WHITE SAUCE

3 tbsp butter, 3 tbsp plain flour (*maida*), 2½ cups milk

¾ tsp salt, ¼ tsp pepper

1. Boil whole tomatoes in water for 3-4 minutes. Cool, peel and blend tomatoes to a smooth puree.

2. Heat olive oil in a pan, add garlic and saute slightly. Add onion and cook till soft and transparent. Add the pureed tomatoes to the onion and stir for a minute. Add the chopped vegetables - carrots, brinjal and zucchini. Mix and add ½ cup water. Cook till the vegetables are soft.

3. Add peas and corn. Stir and add tomato puree, tomato ketchup, salt, oregano, chilli flakes and basil. Cook on low heat till the sauce gets a slightly thick coating consistency. Remove from heat.

4. For the white sauce, melt butter, add flour and stir for a minute. Remove from heat and add milk slowly, stirring constantly with the other hand. Return to heat and cook till you get a sauce of a thin coating consistency.

5. To assemble, butter a 10"x 8" ovenproof dish. Put 1/3 of the red vegetable sauce in the baking dish. Wet the lasagna sheets under running water. Arrange lasagna sheets over the sauce to cover the base of the dish. Break sheets to fill the dish to get a full layer of sheets covering the bottom of the dish.

6. Spread 1/3 of the white sauce over the sheets. Sprinkle both the cheese over the white sauce. Put some red vegetable sauce, then wet some sheets and place on the red sauce. Spread some white sauce and then both the cheese on top. Repeat the red sauce, sheets, white sauce and top with cheese.

7. Cover dish with foil and bake at 190°C for 35 minutes. Remove foil and bake uncovered for 10 minutes to brown the cheese. Serve.

SPINACH & CORN PIE

A pie which is covered with short crust on the top too.

Serves 4-6

SHORT CRUST (BOTTOM AND TOP)
300 gm plain flour (*maida*) - sift with a pinch of salt
150 gm salted butter - cut into thin small slices and chilled, 3-4 tbsp chilled water

FILLING
1 onion - cut into slices
1 bunch spinach (*paalak*) - finely chopped (4½ - 5 cups)
1 cup tinned or frozen corn
50 gm mozzarella, 50 gm cheddar cheese - grated (½ cup of each cheese)
200 gm (¾ cup) yogurt - hang for 30 minutes and squeeze lightly
¾ tsp paprika, 2 tsp cornflour, 1 seasoning cube, 8-9" flan tin (loose bottom low height)

1. Place flour in a bowl. Add butter. Mix the butter into the flour with finger tips till it resembles bread crumbs. Add water and gather into a firm dough. Do not knead too much. Keep aside covered in the fridge for 10-15 minutes.

2. For the filling, heat 2 tbsp oil and onion. Saute for 3-4 minutes till it starts to change colour. Add ½ tsp salt and spinach. Saute for 4-5 minutes on high flame till dry. Add ¾ tsp paprika. Mix cornflour with hung yogurt. Crush seasoning cube and mix with yogurt. Reduce heat. Add yogurt to spinach. Mix well. Add corn. Mix well for 2 minutes till mixture turns dry. Remove from heat. Add both cheeses. Cool the filling completely.

3. Remove dough from fridge and sprinkle dry flour on a rolling board. Divide the dough into 2 balls. Roll a ball thinly between 2 sheets of a polythene. Place it in the tart tin covering the sides too. Do not prick since you are not baking it blind.

4. Spread cooled filling over the tin. Level it and push a little more on the sides. Roll out the second ball of dough thinly. Place on the filling & press the edges to join. Cut away the extra pastry. Press the edges with a fork to get line impression.

5. Cut a cross in the center lightly for the steam to escape.

6. Roll out the left over dough (trimmings of the dough) and cut diamonds to make petals of a flower. Arrange petals around a round centre cut with a small lid (the lid of an essence bottle). Put in a preheated oven at 200°C/400°F for 60 minutes till the upper pastry appears cooked. Remove from oven. Let it cool only for 5 minutes in the tin. If it remains in the tin for longer, it turns soggy. Remove to a wire rack. Let it cool completely. Put it back in the tin and refrigerate.

7. To serve, reheat at 160°C/325°F for 10-15 minutes to heat through.

PEAS & RICE CAKE SIZZLER

Serves 2

PEAS & RICE CAKES

1½ cups boiled rice, 2 tbsp chopped fresh coriander, 1 tbsp oil
1 tsp cumin (*jeera*), 1 tsp chopped ginger, 2 tsp chopped garlic, ½ onion - chopped
1¼ cups boiled or frozen peas, ½ tsp salt or to taste, ½ tsp black pepper
2 slices bread - grind in a mixer to get fresh bread crumbs
¼ tsp salt, or to taste, 1 tbsp fresh coriander

STUFFED TOMATO

2 small firm tomatoes, a pinch of salt and 1 tsp lemon juice, 1 tbsp olive oil or butter
½ tsp finely chopped ginger, ¼ cup chopped carrot, ¼ cup peas (boiled), ¼ cup corn

TO SERVE

BBQ sauce, ready made, 1 tbsp butter, 1-2 cabbage leaves & a few thick onion rings
1 tsp white vinegar, 2 tbsp oil mixed with 1 tbsp water and refrigerated

1. Heat 1 tbsp oil. Add cumin seeds. Let them turn light golden. Add ginger and garlic. Stir for a minute. Add onions and cook for 4-5 minutes on low heat so that they do not turn brown. Add peas, coriander and ½ tsp salt. Cook for 4-5 minutes, sprinkling water in between. Remove from heat. After they cool down, blend to a paste in a grinder. Mix rice, pepper and seasonings with the green peas paste. Add salt to taste. Divide into 4 balls. Flatten balls to get 2" square pieces of 1" height. Dip each in water for a second and roll over bread crumbs mixed with coriander and salt to get a coating. Press well for the bread crumbs to stick. Refrigerate to set.

2. Cut off a slice from tomato to get a narrow opening. Rub a pinch of salt, pepper and ½ tsp of lemon juice in each and keep them inverted. Brush them with a little butter on the outside and inside. For the stuffing, heat 1 tbsp butter. Add ginger and stir. Add carrot and peas. Cover for 5 minutes till carrots turn soft. Mix and add corn and 2 tbsp BBQ sauce. Add ½ tsp salt and a pinch of pepper. Fill both tomatoes with this filling. Heat a pan with 1 tbsp butter. Place the tomatoes in the pan. Turn both carefully to get charred all over. Keep aside.

3. To serve, deep fry the rice cakes on medium heat till crisp and well browned.

4. To assemble sizzler, heat sizzler plate till very hot, put 1 tbsp butter and spread on the iron plate. Reduce heat. Place a cabbage leaf torn into pieces on the hot plate. Place the stuffed tomato on a side. Place a few onion rings if you like.

5. Place 2 rice cakes on it, slightly overlapping. Pour sauce on them and stuffed tomato, taking care not to cover completely. Sprinkle iron plate very lightly with some white vinegar, to sizzle. Put some oil water mix in the wooden tray. Place the hot iron plate on it. Serve.

CANNELLONI IN TANGY TOMATO BASIL SAUCE

Serves 8

12 cannelloni tubes

FILLING

400 gms spinach leaves - chopped (4 cups)
2 tbsp butter, 1 tsp finely chopped garlic, 1 onion - chopped finely
1 cup cream, 200 gms paneer grated, 75 gms (¾ cup) mozzarella cheese
salt & pepper to taste

TANGY TOMATO BASIL SAUCE

1 tbsp butter/olive oil, 500 gms (6-7) tomatoes
1 tbsp garlic chopped finely, 1 onion - chopped finely
1 tsp sugar, 1 tsp salt, ½ tsp chilli powder, 10-12 fresh basil leaves

TOPPING

2½ tbsp butter, 2½ tbsp plain flour (*maida*), 2½ cups milk, ¾ tsp salt, ¼ tsp pepper
100 gms cheddar/parmesan cheese, 2 tsp chopped parsley

1. For the filling, heat butter in a pan, add garlic and onion. Cook till soft. Add the chopped spinach and cook till water evaporates. Add cream and cook for minute. Add paneer, cheese, salt and pepper. Mix. Cool the filling. Wet cannelloni tubes by dipping in water for a second. Stuff the filling into the raw cannelloni tubes.

2. For the sauce, place the tomatoes in a pan. Add 2 cups water and boil the tomatoes for 2-3 minutes. Drain and peel. Chop roughly and cool. Blend tomatoes to a puree. Heat butler/oil in a *kadhai*, add garlic saute for a minute. Add onion and cook till soft. Add the prepared tomato puree and simmer for 5 minutes. Add ¼ cup of water, salt, sugar and chilli powder. Simmer for 1 minute more. Add basil leaves and add to the sauce. Do not overcook the sauce and make it too thick by overcooking.

3. For the white sauce topping, melt butter, add flour and stir for a minute. Remove from heat and add milk slowly, stirring constantly with the other hand. Return to heat and cook till you get a sauce of a thin coating consistency.

4. To assemble, pour the tomato sauce at the bottom of the baking dish. Place the stuffed cannelloni on it. Keep a little space in between each cannelloni for expanding after cooking. Cover them with white sauce. Sprinkle grated cheese and parsley. Put a lid on the baking dish or cover with aluminium foil and bake at 190°C for 30 minutes. For the last 5 minutes, bake uncovered.

SAUTED BABY POTATOES WITH HERBS

Serves 4

500 gms baby potatoes - peeled, see note
2 tbsp butler/oil, 1 tbsp black pepper crushed, 4 tbsp tomato ketchup
½-¾ cup chopped fresh mixed herbs (basil/parsley/mint/coriander/rosemary), use a
combination of any 2-3 fresh herbs that are available

1. Peel the potatoes, prick with fork. Boil 5 cups water with 2 tsp salt. Add potatoes and boil in salted water for 7-8 minutes, or till they get cooked. Check with a knife to see that it goes inside smoothly without any resistance. Drain.

2. Heat oil in a pan for frying. Fry the potatoes. Drain on paper.

3. Heat 2 tbsp butler/oil in a pan. Add crushed pepper, tomato ketchup, mixed herbs and potatoes. Saute to combine spices well. Check salt and add to taste. Serve hot.

Note: If baby potatoes are not available, peel 4-5 large potatoes and scoop out balls with a melon baller to get baby potatoes.

JHATPAT VEGETABLE KORMA

Serves 4

4 baby corns - cut into thick slices, 6 small florets of cauliflower
5-6 French beans - chopped, 1 carrot - diced into ½" pieces
75 gms paneer - cut into ½" pieces
1½ tbsp ghee, 4 cloves (*laung*), 1" piece cinnamon (*dalchini*)
2 green cardamoms (*chhoti illaichi*), ½ tsp cumin seeds (*jeera*)
3 onions - ground to a paste, 2 tsp ginger-garlic-green chilli paste
1 tsp salt, ½ tsp garam masala, ¼ tsp chilli powder, ¼ tsp pepper
½ cup milk, ½ cup coconut milk, 2 tbsp cream

1. Heat ghee, add cloves, cinnamon, cardamoms and cumin seeds. When cumin seeds crackle, add the onion paste and cook till onions turn light golden. Add the ginger-garlic-green chilli paste and cook for a minute. Sprinkle a tbsp water and stir for ½ minute.

2. Add carrot, beans, cauliflower and baby corns. Mix well. Stir for 2-3 minutes. Add salt, garam masala, chilli powder & pepper. Stir to mix well. Add ¼ cup water. Cover & cook on low heat till the vegetables are soft.

3. Add milk, coconut milk, cream and paneer. Cook on low heat for 1-2 minutes. Garnish with coriander leaves and serve hot.

HANDI DAL TARKA

Serves 4

1 cup split red lentils (*dhuli masoor dal*), ¼ cup split yellow lentils (*arhar dal*)
½ tsp turmeric (*haldi*), 1 tsp salt, or to taste, 1 tomato - chopped finely

TEMPERING (*TARKA*)
2-3 tbsp ghee, a pinch of asafoetida (*hing*)
1 tsp cumin seeds & 1 tsp coriander seeds - crushed lightly with a rolling pin (*belan*)
2-3 dry, red chillies - broken, 1 tsp garlic paste, 1 green chilli - chopped finely
1 tsp coriander (*dhania*) powder, ½ tsp garam masala
1 tsp ginger juliennes (match sticks), 2 tbsp green coriander, ½ tsp red chilli powder

1. Wash the dals thoroughly. Put it in a heavy-based sauce pan or a deep pan. Pour 5 cups of water, turmeric and salt. Cover partially and cook on medium heat for about 15 minutes till soft. Mash the dal slightly with a heavy spoon. Add finely chopped tomatoes and simmer for 1-2 minutes.

2. For the tempering, heat ghee. Add cumin and coriander, add garlic and broken red chillies. Stir till garlic starts to change colour. Reduce heat. Add green chilli, coriander powder, garam masala, ginger and green coriander. Mix well and remove from heat. Add red chilli powder. Pour the tempering on the simmering dal. Immediately cover the lid for the flavours to seep into the dal. Serve hot.

77

DUM KI PHOOL GOBHI

Serves 4

1 medium cauliflower (*gobhi*)
2 large onions - sliced very thinly
4 tomatoes - chopped

PASTE

4-5 large flakes garlic, 1" piece ginger
1 tbsp poppy seeds (*khus khus*) & 8 cashewnuts - soaked in hot water for 10 minutes
3" piece fresh coconut - grated

SEASONING

4 tbsp oil, 8 green cardamoms (*chhoti illaichi*) - crushed lightly to open
2" piece cinnamon (*dalchini*), 2 bay leaves (*tej patta*)
1 tsp chilli powder, ½ tsp turmeric (*haldi*), 1 tsp coriander (*dhania*) powder, 1 tsp salt
fresh coriander and slit green chillies - to garnish

1. Cut the cauliflower into large florets. Soak it in 6 cups water with 1 tsp salt for 10 minutes. Drain. Wipe dry on a kitchen towel. Keep aside for 10 minutes to dry.

2. Heat oil in a *kadhai*. Deep fry cauliflower on high heat till light golden. Keep aside. Fry the sliced onions till golden brown and crisp, drain and keep aside.

3. Drain the soaked cashews and poppy seeds. Add fried onions to it. Grind them along with all other ingredients of the paste till smooth. Use a little water for grinding.

4. Heat 4 tbsp oil in a deep *kadhai*, add green cardamoms, cinnamon and bay leaves. Stir for a minute and add the prepared fried onion paste. Stir fry for 2-3 minutes.

5. Add the tomatoes and cook for 4-5 minutes till soft and the masala is well blended. Add the spices - chilli powder, turmeric, coriander powder and salt. Cook for another 2-3 minutes. Add ¼ cup water.

6. Add the cauliflower, stir fry for 2-3 minutes. Reduce heat and cover the *kadhai* with a tight lid. Cook on low flame for 5 minutes till the cauliflower absorbs the flavours. Serve hot.

KHUMB DO PYAZA

A delicious, restaurant style masala preparation of mushrooms.

Serves 4

200 gms mushrooms - each cut into 2 pieces
2 onions - each cut into 4 pieces roughly, 1 tsp ginger chopped, 2-3 flakes garlic
4 tbsp oil/ghee
2 onions - thickly sliced
1 tsp finely chopped ginger, 1 tsp finely chopped garlic
½ cup yogurt - beat well till smooth
¼ tsp turmeric (*haldi*), 2 tsp coriander (*dhania*) powder, 1 tsp salt, or to taste
2 green chillies - slit into 2 pieces lengthwise
2 spring onions - chopped with greens
2 tbsp broken cashewnuts - ground to a paste with ¼ cup water

WHOLE GARAM MASALA (COLLECT TOGETHER)
2 green cardamoms (*chhoti illaichi*), 1 black cardamom (*moti illaichi*)
1" stick cinnamon (*dalchini*), 3-4 cloves (*laung*), 1 bay leaf (*tej patta*)
2 whole dry chillies - each broken into 2 pieces

GARNISH
greens of 1 spring onion - chopped finely
2 tbsp chopped green coriander
2 tsp oil/ghee and ½ tsp red chilli powder for tempering

1. Boil 1 cup water. Add roughly cut onions and boil for 3-4 minutes. Drain water. Blend the boiled onions with ginger and garlic to get a paste.

2. Heat ghee in a *kadhai*, add the collected whole garam masala together and saute over medium heat for 1-2 minutes. Add boiled onion paste and cook for 5-7 minutes on low heat till it starts to change colour and turns golden. Add the thickly sliced onions and cook for 5-6 minutes on medium flame till very light golden.

3. Keeping the heat low, add yogurt, turmeric, salt and coriander powder. Cook till yogurt dries and blends well with the onions. Add 1 tsp each of chopped ginger and garlic. Stir for a minute on low heat.

4. Add cashewnut paste. Mix well. Add mushrooms and cook for 3-4 minutes. Add green chillies. Stir. Add the finely chopped white of spring onion. Lower heat and cook for 3-4 minutes more. Check salt and seasonings.

5. Transfer to a serving dish, garnish with spring onion greens and coriander. Heat 2 tsp oil/ghee in a *kadhai*, remove from heat and add red chilli powder. Pour ghee over mushroom do pyaza. Serve hot.

ACHAARI BROCCOLI & KADU

Serves 4

250 gms pumpkin (*kadu*) - cut in 1" pieces
150 gms (1 medium) broccoli - cut into florets
1 firm tomato - cut into 8 pieces and remove pulp, 4 tbsp oil
2 large onions - chopped roughly, ½ tsp salt, or to taste, ¼ tsp turmeric (*haldi*)
1 tsp coriander (*dhania*) powder, ½ tsp chilli powder, ½ tsp sugar
½ tsp dry mango (*amchoor*) powder

ACHAARI TEMPERING

¾ tsp nigella seeds (*kalonji*), ¼ tsp fenugreek seeds (*methi dana*)
¾ tsp cumin seeds (*jeera*), ¾ tsp mustard seeds (*rai*), ¾ tsp fennel (*saunf*)
2 red chillies - broken in ½" pieces

1. Boil 1½ cups water with ½ tsp salt. Add broccoli and cook for 2 minutes till crisp tender. Remove from water and keep aside.

2. Collect all the achari ingredients for tempering.

3. Heat 4 tbsp oil in a *kadhai* and add the achari ingredients. After a minute, add the onions and cook till light brown.

4. Add salt, turmeric, coriander, chilli powder. Stir for a few seconds. Add pumpkin and stir fry for a minute. Add ¼ cup water. Cover and cook for about 10 minutes till pumpkin is tender but holds its shape.

5. Sprinkle sugar and dry mango powder. Add the broccoli and tomatoes. Mix well for 2-3 minutes and serve hot.

MUGHLAI ALOO MATAR

Serves 4

10 small potatoes or scoop out 10 balls with a melon baller from 2 big potatoes

2 onions - chopped

¾ cup peas - frozen or boiled

4 tbsp oil

1 tsp coriander (*dhania*) powder, ¼ tsp turmeric (*haldi*), ½ tsp red chilli powder

1 tsp cumin seeds (*jeera*) powder, ¾ tsp salt, or to taste

½ cup cream

1 tbsp green coriander, ½ tsp garam masala

PASTE

3 tsp poppy seeds (*khus khus*) - soaked 15 minutes and drained

1 cup thick yogurt

3-4 cashewnuts

5 cloves (*laung*), 4 green cardamoms (*chhoti illaichi*)

4-5 flakes garlic, 1" piece ginger, 4 green chillies - chopped

2 tsp sugar

1. Peel and prick the potatoes, soak them in hot water for 15-20 minutes to which 1 tsp salt is added.

2. Drain poppy seeds & make a paste with all the other ingredients of the paste.

3. Marinate the potatoes in the yogurt paste.

4. Heat oil in a *kadhai*, add chopped onions and stir till golden brown. Add coriander, red chilli, turmeric, cumin powder and salt. Cook for a minute.

5. Add the marinated potatoes along with the yogurt and stir for 3-4 minutes. Reduce heat, add 2½ cups of water. Cover and simmer till the potatoes are soft and cooked properly.

6. Add peas, cream, garam masala and coriander leaves. Serve hot.

METHI PANEER

Serves 3-4

1 bunch (500 gms) fenugreek greens (*methi*) - chop leaves finely
100 gms paneer - cut into tiny pieces, ½ tsp cumin seeds (*jeera*)
2 dried red chillies - broken, 1 tsp finely chopped ginger, 1 large onion - chopped finely
1 tsp coriander (*dhania*) powder, ¼ tsp turmeric (*haldi*)
½ tsp salt to taste, ½ tsp garam masala
2 tomatoes - chopped finely, ¼ cup cream, ¼ cup milk

1. Boil 4 cups water with 2 tsp sugar and 2 tsp salt in a *kadhai*. Add the fenugreek greens leaves and boil for 5-6 minutes on low heat till soft. Drain, refresh in cold water and keep aside.

2. Heat oil in a *kadhai*. Add cumin seeds, broken red chillies & chopped ginger. Stir and add the onions. Cook till light brown. Add coriander powder, turmeric, salt and garam masala. Stir for a minute.

3. Add the tomatoes and cook for 3-4 minutes. Add ½ cup water, cover and simmer the masala on low heat till well blended.

4. Add the boiled fenugreek greens and stir fry the fenugreek greens for 5-6 minutes. Add cream and paneer, mix well. Add the milk & adjust the seasonings. Serve hot.

LAUKI AUR MATAR MILAN

Serves 4

½ of a small bottle gourd (*lauki*) (total weight of gourd 250 gm) – cut piece into half
lengthwise & then cut into ¾" thick slices (1 cup)
1 cup peas
3 tbsp oil, 1 tsp cumin seeds (*jeera*)
1 tbsp garlic paste, ½ tsp ginger paste

MASALA
1 tbsp oil, 1 dry red chilli
2 onions - chopped finely
1 tsp salt, 2 tsp coriander (*dhania*) powder
¼ tsp turmeric (*haldi*), ¼ tsp red chilli powder
1 tsp garlic paste
1½ tomatoes - chopped finely, 3-4 tbsp tomato puree

GRIND TOGETHER
1 tsp fennel (*saunf*), 2 green cardamoms (*chhoti illaichi*)
¼ tsp carom seeds (*ajwain*)

1. Boil gourd in 8 cups water with 1½ tsp salt for 10 minutes till soft. Strain. Refresh in cold water.

2. Heat 2 tbsp oil. Add 1 tsp cumin seeds. When it turns golden, add 1 tbsp garlic paste and ½ tsp ginger paste. Stir for a minute. Add boiled gourd. Saute for 2-3 minutes. Add peas, stir fry for 2 minutes on high heat. Remove from fire.

3. For the masala, heat 1 tbsp oil. Add 1 broken red chilli. Wait for a minute till it starts to darken. Add onions and cook till light brown. Add 1 tsp salt, 2 tsp coriander powder, ¼ tsp turmeric, ¼ tsp red chilli powder and 1 tsp garlic paste. Cook for about 2 minutes till onions turn brown.

4. Add chopped tomatoes. Stir well. Add 3-4 tbsp tomato puree. Cook on low heat for 5-7 minutes.

5. Add the above vegetables to the masala. Mix well.

6. Add ground fennel, green cardamoms and carom seeds. Toss lightly and serve.

STUFFED ALOO LAJAWAB

Serves 10

4 medium potatoes
oil for frying

FILLING

50 gm paneer and 50 gm khoya or 100 gm paneer - crumbled
1 green chilli - finely chopped, 3 tbsp chopped coriander leaves, ½ tsp salt
½ tsp cumin (*jeera*) powder, ½ tsp coriander (*dhania*) powder, ¼ tsp garam masala

GRAVY

4 tbsp oil
2 large onions - ground to a paste
½ tsp red chilli powder, 1½ tsp salt, 1 tsp cumin seeds (*jeera*) powder
4 tbsp khoya, ½ cup cream
3 green cardamoms (*chhoti illaichi*), 3 cloves (*laung*) - grind together to a powder

PASTE -1 (GRIND TOGETHER)

2 tomatoes, ½ tsp garlic paste, 1 tsp ginger paste, 2 green chillies - chopped

PASTE - 2 (GRIND TOGETHER)

1 tbsp poppy seeds (*khus khus*), 6-8 cashews (*kaju*), ½ cup curd

1. Peel the potatoes. With a peeler scoop out the centre to get a hollow for the filling. Let the opening not be too broad.

2. Mix all the ingredients of the filling and keep aside.

3. Heat oil for frying in a *kadhai* and fry the hollow potatoes in oil on low medium heat till they turn golden and get cooked. Remove from oil.

4. Stuff the paneer filling into the potatoes and press well. Keep aside.

5. For the gravy, heat 4 tbsp oil in a *kadhai*, add onion paste and cook till golden brown. Add dry masalas - salt, cumin powder and red chilli powder. Stir for a few seconds and add ¼ cup water.

6. Add 1st paste (tomato-ginger-garlic & green chilli paste). Cook till paste dries.

7. Add 2nd paste (poppy seeds, cashews & curd), cook for 3-4 minutes on low heat.

8. Add 1 cup water. Bring to a boil. Simmer on low heat for 4-5 minutes. Add the khoya and cream. Stir well. Grind cardamom and cloves to a powder and sprinkle over the gravy. Keep aside.

9. To serve, cut the potatoes into ½" thick slices. Put the gravy in a low sided dish and top with potatoes. Heat in a microwave to serve.

RAJASTHANI GATTA CURRY

Serves 6-8

GATTAS
2 cups (200 gms) gram flour (*besan*)
3 tbsp oil
2 tbsp yogurt
1 tsp salt
1 tsp chilli powder
½ tsp coriander (*dhania*) powder
¼ tsp turmeric (*haldi*), ¼ tsp garam masala
pinch of soda-bi-carb, 1 tbsp finely chopped coriander

CURRY
4 tbsp oil
a pinch of asafoetida (*hing*), ½ tsp cumin seeds (*jeera*)
½ tsp coriander seeds (*saboot dhania*)
3 onions - grated
3 tomatoes, 1" piece ginger, 6-8 flakes garlic
1 tsp coriander (*dhania*) powder, ½ tsp chilli powder
½ tsp garam masala, 1 tsp salt, a pinch of turmeric (*haldi*)
½ cup curd - beat well to make it smooth

1. For the gattas, sift gram flour. Add oil, yogurt, salt, chilli, coriander powder, turmeric, soda-bi-carb, garam masala and coriander leaves to the gram flour. Add a little water and knead into a tight dough. (Knead the dough well).

2. Divide the dough into 5-6 balls and roll into long, ½" thick rolls. Cut each roll into ½" small slices.

3. Boil 2 cups of water in a pan, immerse the small gatta pieces in boiling water and boil on low flame for 2-3 minutes. On getting cooked, gatta's will get light in colour. Drain and reserve the water.

4. For the curry, make a paste of tomatoes, garlic and ginger. Heat oil in a *kadhai*, add asafoetida and cumin seeds and slightly crushed coriander seeds, stir and add the grated onions. Cook till light brown. Add the prepared tomato paste and cook again till thick and oil separates a little.

5. Add all the masalas and salt. Reduce heat. Mix well and add the yogurt, stirring constantly. Add the gatta's and the reserved water. Add 1 more cup of water and bring to a boil. Simmer for 2-3 minutes. Remove from heat and garnish with coriander leaves. Serve hot.

MAKAI MOOLI KI BHAAJI

Serves 6

150 gms babycorns - sliced into half and cut into 1" pieces
2 medium sized radish (*mooli*) with green tops - chop 1 radish finely and cut the other
radish into ¼" thick slices, chop the greens of both or use greens of even 3 radish
3 tbsp oil, ¼ tsp nigella seeds (*kalonji*), ½ tsp cumin seeds (*jeera*)
2 medium onions - chopped finely
1 tsp coriander (*dhania*) powder, ½ tsp chilli powder, ¼ tsp turmeric (*haldi*)
½ tsp salt or to taste, 1 tsp ginger or garlic - chopped finely
1 green chilli - chopped finely, 2 tomatoes - chopped finely, ½ tsp *anaardana* powder

1. Boil 2 cups water with 1 tsp salt and ¼ tsp turmeric. Add the babycorns and boil for 2-3 minutes. Drain. Keep aside.

2. Heat oil in a *kadhai*, add nigella and cumin seeds, wait till cumin turns light golden. Add the onions and cook till light golden. Add ginger or garlic and green chillies.

3. Add chopped and sliced radish. Cook for 3-4 minutes. Add the greens. Add coriander powder, turmeric, chilli powder and salt. Cook on low flame for 5-6 minutes till radish turns soft and dry.

4. Add tomatoes and babycorns. Add *anaardana*. Mix well for 3-4 minutes. Add ½ cup water. Cover & simmer on low heat till masala is well blended. Serve.

KHATTA METHA DAKSHINI BAINGAN

Serves 4

500 gms small brinjals (*baigans*) - slit into 4 pieces half way
oil for frying

PASTE
3 tbsp grated fresh coconut
5-6 pepper corns (*saboot kali mirch*)
½ tsp cumin seeds (*jeera*)
1 tsp coriander seeds (*saboot dhania*)
½ tsp mustard seeds (*rai*)

OTHER INGREDIENTS
2 tbsp tamarind (*imli*) - soaked in ½ cup water
1 tbsp jaggery (*gur*)/brown sugar
10-15 curry leaves
1 small onion - chopped
1 tomato - chopped
½ tsp mustard seeds (*rai*)
2-3 tbsp oil
¼ tsp black pepper powder and salt to taste

1. Rub a pinch of chilli powder and salt in each brinjal and keep aside for 10 minutes.

2. Heat a non stick pan, dry roast coconut till light brown, remove from heat. Dry roast pepper corns, cumin seeds, coriander seeds & mustard seeds together till cumin seeds turns golden and fragrant. Cool and blend coconut with all the other spices to a smooth paste by adding a little water. Keep aside.

3. Heat oil in a *kadhai* for frying. Deep fry the brinjals on medium heat till light brown and cooked. Remove on a paper napkin and keep aside.

4. Heat 2 tbsp oil in a *kadhai*, splutter mustard seeds, add curry leaves, stir for a minute. Add onions and cook till light golden, add tomatoes and cook till soft.

5. Add the prepared coconut paste and cook well for 2-3 minutes.

6. Add 4 tbsp tamarind pulp and jaggery, stir add salt and pepper powder.

7. Add ½ cup water to get a masala which coats the brinjals. Bring to a boil and stir for a minute. Add fried brinjals, mix well. Cook covered for 2-3 minutes till masala coats the brinjals. Serve.

PANEER CHANDANI

Serves 4-6

250 gms paneer - cut into square pieces, 2 tbsp ghee or oil
1 green cardamom (*chhoti illaichi*), 2-3 cloves (*laung*), 1" stick cinnamon (*dalchini*)
1 small onion - finely chopped, ¼ tsp white pepper ½ tsp salt or to taste, ½ cup milk

CHANDINI PASTE
12 whole or 3 tbsp broken cashewnuts - soaked for 5-10 minutes
1" piece ginger - chopped (2 tbsp), 2 green chillies, 3 green cardamoms (*chhoti illaichi*)
100 gms (½ cup) fresh khoya

GARNISH
3-4 strands saffron (*kesar*) - soaked 1 tbsp milk

1. For the chandani paste, place cashewnuts, ginger, green chillies and green cardamoms in a small mixer. Add a little water and grind to a smooth paste. Add khoya to the mixer. Add about ½ cup water again and blend to a smooth paste. Keep aside.

2. Melt 2 tbsp ghee or oil in a non stick *kadhai*. Add green cardamoms, cloves, cinnamon on low flame. After a minute, add the onions and cook for 3-4 minutes on very low flame till the onion are soft, stirring constantly. Make sure that they do not brown as it will discolour the gravy.

3. Add the prepared chandani paste and cook on low heat stirring constantly, so that it does not stick to the bottom. Add ¼ cup water. Cook for 7-8 minutes till you get a thick gravy. Add pepper and salt. Add milk, add the paneer and cook for 2-3 minutes to warm through. Remove from heat. Remove to serving bowl, garnish with soaked kesar and green coriander leaves.

BALTI MAKAI PALAK

Serves 4

1 bundle (600 gm) spinach (*palak*) - cut into thin long shreds
100 gms babycorns - cut into half lengthwise, 1 tbsp lemon juice
1 tsp sugar, 1 tsp salt, a pinch of turmeric (*haldi*)
3-4 tbsp oil, ½ tsp cumin seeds (*jeera*), 1 tbsp finely chopped garlic
2 dry, red chillies - broken, 1 large onion - cut into rings, 1 tomato - finely chopped
¾ tsp salt or to taste, 1 tsp coriander (*dhania*) powder, ½ tsp garam masala

CRUSH TOGETHER
1 clove (*laung*) and 1 green cardamom (*chhoti illaichi*)

1. Wash the spinach nicely. Place in a strainer and squeeze out excess water.

2. Heat 3 cups water in a pan. Add lemon juice, sugar, 1 tsp salt and a pinch of turmeric. Bring to a boil and add babycorns. Boil for 1-2 minutes. Strain.

3. Heat oil in a wok or a large *kadhai*. Add cumin seeds. Let it turn golden. Add garlic, red chillies and onion rings. Stir for ½ minute till garlic changes colour.

4. Add the spinach and salt. Stir fry till dry and well fried. Add garam masala and coriander powder.

5. Add the baby corns and tomatoes, cook for 4-5 minutes till tomatoes are slightly soft and spinach blends with the baby corns. Serve hot.

Note: You may use 1½ cups of frozen corn instead of baby corns.

BHINDI DO PYAAZA

Two forms of onions - sliced and big chunks. A little tomato puree binds the vegetable.

Serves 4-6

500 gms lady fingers (*bhindi*) - cut into 1" pieces diagonally, 4-5 tbsp oil
½ tsp cumin seeds (*jeera*), 2 onions - thinly sliced
1 onion - cut into 8 pieces and separated
¼ tsp turmeric (*haldi*), 1 tsp chilli powder, 1 tsp salt, 4 tbsp tomato puree

GRIND TOGETHER

2 tsp fennel (*saunf*), 1 tbsp coriander seeds (saboot dhania), 1 tsp cumin seeds (*jeera*)

1. Grind together fennel, coriander seeds and cumin seeds in a small spice grinder to a powder. Keep aside.

2. Heat oil in a large flat *kadhai* or wok, add ½ tsp cumin seeds and let them turn golden. Add sliced onions and stir till soft and transparent, for about 3-4 minutes.

3. Add lady fingers. Stir for 2-3 minutes. Cover and cook on low heat for about 10 minutes till the lady fingers is soft. Keep stirring in between.

4. Add the onion pieces and cook for 2 minutes.

5. Add the prepared fennel powder, turmeric, chilli powder, salt and mix well for 2-3 minutes.

6. Add the tomato puree. Mix well for 2 minutes and serve hot.

PANEER CORN TAKA TAK

Serves 6

2 tbsp butter, 1½ tbsp oil
6 large tomatoes - grind to a puree in a mixer, 1 tsp salt, 1 tsp chilli powder, ½ tsp sugar
2 small onions - cut into rings, 1 cup corn (boiled or frozen)
1 capsicum - cut into 1" pieces
200 gms paneer - cut into 1" pieces, 1 tsp kasoori methi, 2-3 tbsp cream

1. Heat 2 tbsp butter in a *kadhai*. Add freshly ground tomatoes. Cook till dry. Add salt, chilli powder & sugar. Cook for 2-3 minutes on low heat. Keep aside.

2. Heat 1½ tbsp oil in a non stick wok or a large non stick pan . Add onion rings and saute till soft. Add corn and capsicum. Saute for a minute.

3. Add paneer and the prepared tomato masala. Mix well.

4. Add ½ cup water and kasoori methi. Simmer till well blended.

5. Add cream and mix well. Remove from heat. Serve hot.

VEGETABLES IN METHI CURRY

Serves 4

1 cup peas - boiled or frozen

1 cup carrot diced into small pieces

1 cup chopped fresh fenugreek greens (*methi*)

3 tbsp oil

½ tsp cumin seeds (*jeera*)

1 onion - chopped finely

½ tsp red chilli, 1 tsp coriander (*dhania*) powder, 1½ tsp salt

¼ tsp garam masala

1 tbsp dry fenugreek leaves (*kasoori methi*), 2-3 tbsp cream

1 tsp ginger juliennes

PASTE (GRIND TOGETHER)

2 tomatoes - chopped, 10 cashewnuts

5-6 flakes garlic

1" piece ginger

1. Boil 2 cups water with ½ tsp sugar. Add carrots and peas. Boil for 2 minutes till carrots are crisp-tender. Remove from water with a strainer. Add ½ tsp sugar to the boiling water. Add fenugreek and boil for 3-4 minutes till soft. Strain fenugreek and squeeze out the excess water. Keep vegetables aside.

2. Heat oil in a *kadhai*, add cumin seeds and let it turn golden. Add the onion and stir fry till light brown.

3. Add chilli powder, coriander powder and salt. Mix well for a few seconds. Add the prepared tomato-cashew paste and cook for 4-5 minutes till dry.

4. Squeeze and add the fenugreek greens and bhuno for 3-4 minutes. Add carrots and peas. Mix well. Add 2 cups of water and bring to a boil. Boil for 2 minutes.

5. Reduce heat. Add garam masala, dry fenugreek leaves and cream. Garnish with ginger juliennes and serve hot.

DAL MAKHANI

Serves 4-5

1 cup whole black beans (*urad saboot*)
2 tbsp split gram lentils (*channe ki dal*)
5 cups of water
2 tbsp desi ghee, 1½ tsp salt
¾ cup milk, 1 cup ready-made tomato puree
¼ tsp nutmeg (*jaiphal*) powder, ½ tsp garam masala
1½ tbsp dry fenugreek leaves (*kasoori methi*)
1 tsp tomato ketchup
1 tsp tandoori masala (optional)
2-3 tbsp butter, preferably white

GRIND TO A PASTE

2 dry, whole red chillies - deseeded & soaked for 10 minutes and then drained
1½ tsp chopped ginger, 2 tsp chopped garlic

ADD LATER

½ cup cream
¼ tsp garam masala, a pinch of red colour (optional)

1. Wash dals, and soak in warm water for at least 2-3 hours.

2. Drain water. Wash several times in fresh water, rubbing well, till the water no longer remains black.

3. Pressure cook dal with 5 cups water, 2 tbsp ghee, salt and ginger-garlic-chilli paste. After the first whistle, keep on low flame for 25-30 minutes. Remove from fire.

4. After the pressure drops, nicely whisk the hot dal and hot milk together using a whisk. Add tomato puree, nutmeg, garam masala, dry fenugreek leaves, ketchup and tandoori masala.

5. Add butter. Simmer on medium flame for 20-25 minutes, stirring dal occasionally. Remove from fire. Keep aside to cool till the time of serving.

6. At the time of serving, add cream and milk to the dal. Keep dal on fire and bring to a boil on low heat, stirring constantly. Mix very well with a karchhi. Simmer for 2 minutes more, to get the right colour and smoothness. Remove from fire. Sprinkle garam masala and colour. Mix and serve.

Note: Originally the dal was cooked by leaving it overnight on the burning coal angithis. The longer the dal simmered, the better it tasted.

MIXED VEGETABLES

Serves 6

3 small carrots - half lengthwise and then cut into ½" thick slices
½ of a small bottle gourd (*lauki*) - cut into ½" cubes (1 cup)
4-5 big florets of broccoli or cauliflower
¼ of a small medium cabbage - cut into 1" squares (1½ cups)
½ cup corn, ½ cup peas, 3 tbsp oil, 1 tsp cumin seeds (*jeera*)
1 tbsp garlic paste, ½ tsp ginger paste
½ tsp salt, ½ tsp turmeric (*haldi*) & ¾ tsp red chilli, 1 tsp cumin seeds (*jeera*) powder

MASALA

1 tbsp oil, 2 onions - chopped finely
1 tsp salt, 3 tsp coriander (*dhania*) powder
¼ tsp turmeric (*haldi*), ¼ tsp red chilli powder
1 tsp garlic paste
1½ tomatoes - chopped finely, 5 tbsp tomato puree

GRIND TOGETHER

1 tsp fennel (*saunf*), 2 green cardamoms, ¼ tsp carom seeds (*ajwain*)

1. Boil carrot and bottle gourd in salted water for 5-7 minutes till soft. Add broccoli or cauliflower florets and boil for 2 minutes. Strain. Refresh in cold water.

2. Heat 3 tbsp oil. Add 1 tsp cumin seeds. When they turn golden, add 1 tbsp garlic paste and ½ tsp ginger paste. Add blanched broccoli or cauliflower. Saute for 1 minute. Add carrot and bottle gourd. Stir and add salt, turmeric and red chilli powder. Saute for 2-3 minutes. Add cabbage stir fry for 5 minutes on high heat till cabbage turns slightly soft.

3. For the masala, heat 1 tbsp oil. Add onions and cook till light brown. Add 1 tsp salt, 3 tsp coriander powder, ¼ tsp turmeric, ¼ tsp red chilli powder and 1 tsp garlic paste. Cook for about 2 minutes till onions blend well with the masala.

4. Add chopped tomatoes. Stir well. Add 5 tbsp tomato puree. Cook on low heat for 5-7 minutes.

5. Add corn and peas. Add the above vegetables also. Mix well.

6. Add ground fennel, green cardamoms and carom seeds. Toss lightly and serve.

BHINDI ALOO KA SALAN

A spicy Hyderabadi curry. Add any vegetable of your choice to the curry & enjoy with rice.

Serves 4-6

250 gms small lady fingers (*bhindi*), keeping it whole, make a slit
2 potatoes - each cut into 4 pieces lengthwise and then into thin slices
6-8 green chillies - slit slightly (so they do not burst while frying)
4 tbsp oil, 1 tsp cumin seeds (*jeera*), ¼ tsp fenugreek seeds (*methi dana*)
½ tsp mustard seeds (*rai*), ¼ tsp nigella seed (*kalonji*), 6-8 curry leaves
¼ tsp turmeric (*haldi*), 2 tsp chilli powder, 1 tsp coriander (*dhania*) powder, 1½ tsp salt
a small lemon size ball of tamarind - soak to get 4 tbsp tamarind pulp
¼ cup chopped coriander leaves

DRY ROAST AND GRIND TO POWDER
2 tbsp peanuts, 2 tbsp sesame seeds (*til*)
1 tbsp cumin seeds (*jeera*), 2 dry, red *Kashmiri* chillies

GRIND TO A PASTE
1 large onion - chopped, 2 tomatoes - chopped
1" piece ginger, 6-8 flakes garlic, 3 tbsp grated coconut (fresh)

1. Heat oil in a *kadhai*, fry lady fingers on high heat for 3-4 minutes till soft and green . Do not let it turn brown and do not fry on low heat as it will turn chewy on doing so. Remove lady fingers from oil and add the potatoes to the oil. Fry on medium low heat till light golden and cooked. Shut off the flame. Add green chillies and fry till whitish patches appear on them. Remove all vegetables from oil on paper napkins to absorb excess oil.

2. Dry roast peanuts, sesame seeds, cumin seeds & red chillies in a non stick pan till sesame seeds turn golden brown. Cool & grind together to a very fine powder.

3. Make a smooth paste with all the ingredients of the paste. Keep aside.

4. Heat oil in a *kadhai*. Add cumin seeds, fenugreek seeds, carom seeds and nigella seeds. Wait till fenugreek seeds turn golden brown. Add curry leaves. Wait for a minute.

5. Add the ground tomato paste and cook for 8-10 minutes till well cooked, dry and oil separates. Add turmeric, chilli powder, coriander powder and salt.

6. Add the ground powder (from step 2) and cook again on medium flame for 1 minute.

7. Add 2½ cups of water, bring to a boil. Give 2-3 boils. Add 4 tbsp tamarind pulp. Keep curry aside.

8. To serve, heat curry. Add the fried vegetables and simmer for 1-2 minutes. Add coriander leaves and serve hot with steamed rice.

BROWN CORIANDER RICE

Unpolished brown rice is very healthy though a little chewy. It takes more water to cook. Try acquiring the taste of this fibre rich rice.

Serves 4

1 cup brown rice - wash and soak for 15 minutes
200 gms spinach (*paalak*) - chopped, washed & drained well (2 cups)
1 cup grated carrot, ½ cup corn
1 large onion - sliced finely
1½ tsp salt
3 tbsp oil

CORIANDER PASTE
½ cup chopped coriander, 1 tsp chopped ginger
2 green chillies, 5-6 flakes garlic
2 green cardamoms (*chhoti illaichi*)
2 cloves (*laung*)
2 tbsp water to grind

1. Wash rice and keep aside.

2. Grind all the ingredients of the paste. Keep aside.

3. Heat oil. Add onion. Cook till golden brown.

4. Add the coriander paste, cook for 2-3 minutes on low flame.

5. Add chopped spinach, corn and carrot. Stir on high flame till dry.

6. Add rice and 3 cups water. Add salt. Mix. Bring to a good boil.

7. Cover the pan of rice with a well fitting lid. Cook on very low heat for about 22-25 minutes till the rice is done and the water gets absorbed.

SUBZ PARDA BIRYANI

Serves 4

PARDA
1 cup plain flour (*maida*), 2 tbsp ghee, ¾ tsp salt
½ cup milk, approx. to maka a dough of rolling consistency

VEGETABLE LAYER
4 tbsp ghee, 3 onions - sliced finely, 2 tbsp ginger-garlic paste
1 cup diced carrots (¼" cubes), ½ cup chopped beans
1 cup small florets of cauliflower, ½ cup peas, 1 cup thick yogurt, 1¾ tsp salt, or to taste

GRIND TO A POWDER
2" piece cinnamon, 3-4 cloves, 5 green cardamoms, 1 blade mace (*javitri*)

RICE LAYER
2 cups rice, 4 green cardamoms, 1 bay leaf, 2 whole star anise, 2 tsp salt

FLAVOURING
¼ cup warm milk mixed with 2 drops of kewra essence & a few strands of saffron (*kesar*)
1 onion - sliced and deep fried till crisp, ¼ cup mint, 2 tbsp melted butter or ghee

1. For the parda, mix plain flour with ghee & salt. Knead very well, using milk to make a smooth roti dough. Keep aside covered for 1 hour with a cling wrap.

2. For the vegetable layer, heat ghee in a pan, add sliced onions and saute till brown. Add ginger-garlic paste and the ground spice powder. Stir for a few seconds. Add vegetables, stir for 5 minutes on medium flame. Reduce heat and add the yogurt slowly, stirring constantly. Stir till yogurt dries and coats the vegetables. Add 1 cup water. Cover and cook on low heat till vegetables are crisp tender. Mix salt. Remove from heat. (The vegetable mixture should not be dry, it should have some gravy).

3. For the rice layer, boil 10 cups water with all the spices and salt in a large pan. Add rice and boil till soft but firm. Drain and spread in a large tray to cool slightly and evaporate the steam. Fluff with a fork in between.

4. To assemble the biryani, take a dish or handi which will fit in your oven. Put half of the cooked vegetables in it & cover vegetables with rice. Sprinkle milk to which kewra and saffron has been added. Sprinkle some fried onions & mint. Repeat the vegetable & then rice layer. Sprinkle the gravy of the vegetables on the rice. Spread onion-mint layer. Dot with 1 tbsp of melted butter or ghee.

5. For the parda, put some flour on the kitchen platform, roll out the dough thinly, slightly larger than the mouth of the handi or dish. Place roti on the dish or handi and seal the edges. Apply melted ghee or butter on top. Put the rice in the oven for 20-30 minutes at 160°C till the dough is light golden in colour and well cooked. To serve, cut the parda from the centre.

JHATPAT SUBZ BIRYANI

Serves 4-6

2 cups basmati rice
1 bay leaf (*tej patta*), 1 onion - sliced
¾ tsp ginger paste, 2 tsp garlic paste
7-8 beans - cut into ¾"
1 potato - cut into cubes and boiled with lemon juice
½ carrot - cut into cubes and boiled with lemon juice
3 tbsp tomato puree
½ tsp red chilli powder, ¼ tsp turmeric (*haldi*), 1 tsp salt
2 tbsp fresh mint, 2 tbsp dry mint - crushed
1 tbsp lemon juice
5 tbsp oil

BIRYANI MASALA

4-5 pepper corns (*saboot kali mirch*), 2 green cardamoms (*chhoti illaichi*)
1" cinnamon (*dalchini*), 2 cloves (*laung*)
½ tsp cumin seeds (*jeera*)

1. For the rice layer, boil 10 cups water with 2 tsp salt in a large pan. Add rice and boil till soft but firm. Drain and spread in a large tray to cool slightly and evaporate the steam. Fluff with a fork in between. Keep aside.

2. Grind all spices of the biryani masala to a powder. Keep aside.

3. Heat oil. Add bay leaf. Stir. Add onion and cook till golden.

4. Add ginger-garlic paste. Sprinkle some water.

5. Add ½ of the freshly prepared biryani masala.

6. Add beans and stir for 3-4 minutes till half cooked. Add boiled carrots and potatoes. Saute for 4-5 minutes.

7. Add tomato puree. Stir. Add turmeric, salt and red chilli powder. Stir for 2-3 minutes.

8. Add fresh poodina. Mix well.

9. Add rice and stir for 4-5 minutes.

10. Add lemon juice and dry mint. Mix well.

METHI NA THEPLA

Serves 4

2 cups (250 gms) whole wheat flour (*atta*)
2½ cups chopped fresh fenugreek greens (*methi*)
¼ cup gram flour (*besan*), ¼ tsp turmeric (*haldi*), ½ tsp sesame seeds (*til*)
1 tsp sugar
½ tsp salt to taste
1 tbsp grated ginger, 2 green chillies - chopped
½ cup yogurt, 1 tbsp oil
oil or ghee for frying

1. Wash the chopped fenugreek greens.

2. Mix whole wheat flour with fenugreek greens, gram flour, turmeric, sesame seeds, sugar, salt, ginger and chillies.

3. Add yogurt and oil, knead into a semi hard dough, adding enough water. Keep aside covered for 30 minutes.

4. Divide the dough in equal size balls, roll each into a round shape of 5" diameter.

5. Cook on medium hot *tawa* on both sides, smear ghee on each side and serve hot.

BAKHAR KHANI

Makes 4

2 cups plain flour (*maida*), 4 tbsp ghee
1½ tsp soda-bi-carb (*mitha soda*), pinch of baking powder, 1 tbsp sugar and ½ tsp salt
seeds of 4-6 green cardamoms (*chhoti illaichi*) - crushed
½ cup milk, approx. - enough to make a dough
1 drop of kewra essence

1. Sift flour with soda and baking powder. Add all other ingredients and knead with enough milk to get a dough of rolling consistency. Knead well and keep covered overnight.

2. Make 4 balls. Roll each ball into a roti of ½" thickness and lightly make check incisions, without cutting through.

3. Cook on medium heat on a thick bottom *tawa* till cooked through. Add ghee and fry till crisp.

Note: (Add only 1 drop kewra essence, as it is a strong essence. Drop the essence on a spoon and mix with the milk to make the dough).

CARROT PARANTHA

Serves 4

2 cups grated carrot, 2 tbsp oil, 1/8 tsp asafoetida (*hing*), ½ tsp cumin seeds (*jeera*)
2 tbsp gram flour (*besan*), 1 tsp salt, 2 tsp chilli powder
1 green chilli - chopped, ¼ cup green coriander - chopped

DOUGH

1¼ cups whole wheat flour (*atta*), 1 tbsp oil, ½ tsp salt

1. Squeeze the grated carrots and keep the squeezed juice aside.

2. Heat 2 tbsp oil in a non stick pan, add asafoetida and cumin. Stir and add the gram flour. Stir and add the grated carrots and cook on low heat till gram flour blends well with the carrots. Add salt and chilli powder. Remove from heat, mix green chillies and coriander. Keep carrot stuffing aside.

3. In the flour, add 1 tbsp oil, salt and carrot juice. Mix and add enough water to make a soft dough. Keep covered for 30 minutes. Divide the dough into 6 balls. Roll each ball into a small roti, place one portion of carrot stuffing and close it from all sides. Roll again to make a stuffed parantha. Shallow fry in oil. Serve hot.

MATAR KA PARANTHA

Serves 6

dough prepared from 2 cups whole wheat flour (*atta*)

FILLING

2 cups green peas (raw), 1 tbsp finely chopped ginger, 2 green chillies, ¼ cup green coriander
2 tbsp oil, a pinch of asafoetida (*hing*), 1 tsp nigella seed (*kalonji*), 1 tsp fennel (*saunf*)
½ tsp coriander seeds (*saboot dhania*) - crushed coarsely, 1 tsp salt

1. Grind peas, ginger, green chillies, coriander in a mixer-grinder to a coarse paste.

2. Heat oil in a non stick pan, add asafoetida, nigella seeds, fennel and coriander seeds. Stir and add the peas paste. Add salt and cook for 1-2 minute till the paste turns slightly thick and sticks together. Remove from heat.

3. Make balls from the dough. Roll out each and put 2 tbsp of peas filling in the centre. Collect dough from all sides to cover the filling. Flatten and roll into a parantha. Shallow fry with oil, serve hot with a thin potato curry.

MATAR KI POORI

2 cups plain flour (*maida*), 2 tbsp semolina (*suji*), 2 tbsp oil and ½ tsp salt

1. Add enough water to the above ingredients to make a stiff dough. Keep aside.

2. Make pooris of this dough, filling them with the peas filling as given above.

PALAK-PANEER PARANTHAS

Makes 7-8

2 cups (250 gms) whole wheat flour (*atta*)
1 tbsp vinegar, ½ tsp salt, 4 tbsp (50 gms) softened butter

FILLING

400 gms spinach (*paalak*) - keep leaves and discard stalk
2 tsp oil, ¼ tsp carom seeds (*ajwain*), 1 small onion
1 tsp garlic - crushed & chopped, 1 green chilli - chopped
100 gms paneer - grated (½ cup), ½ tsp salt, or to taste

1. Combine flour, vinegar, salt and enough water to knead into a dough of rolling consistency. Let the dough rest for 2 hours, then fold in butter into the dough and knead again. Keep aside.

2. For the filling, boil 3 cups of water in a pan. Add the spinach leaves and remove from heat. Leave the spinach in hot water for ½ minute. Strain spinach and refresh under cold water in a strainer. Squeeze out excess water. Chop finely.

3. Heat 2 tsp oil. Add carom seeds, onion and garlic. Stir and add chopped spinach & green chilli. Stir for 2 minutes. Add paneer and salt. Mix and remove from heat.

4. To make the paranthas, divide the dough into 7-8 balls. Roll out each ball into a small circle, place the filling in the center and collect from all sides to enclose the filling. Press over dry flour and roll into medium sized paranthas. Heat a thick bottom *tawa*. Cook paranthas on both sides on medium heat. Spread 1 tsp of butter on one side and cook till crisp. Serve hot.

KATHAL KI BIRYANI

Serves 4-6

2 cups basmati rice - wash and soak for 10 minutes
½ kg jack fruit (*kathal*) - cut into small pieces
3 large onions - sliced
4 tbsp oil
1 tsp cumin seeds (*jeera*), 2 bay leaves (*tej patta*)
4-5 green cardamoms (*chhoti illaichi*), 2 black cardamoms (*moti illaichi*)
2" stick cinnamon (*dalchini*), 4-5 cloves (*laung*)
2 tbsp ginger-garlic-green chilli paste
1 tbsp coriander (*dhania*) powder, salt to taste
1 tsp ground biryani masala, see note
¼ cup mint (*poodina*) leaves
¼ cup warm milk mixed with 2-3 drops kewra essence and 6-7 strands of saffron
oil for frying

1. Heat oil in a *kadhai*, deep fry the kathal pieces till golden brown, remove on paper napkins. In the same oil, fry the onions till golden brown. Remove from oil and keep crisp fried onions aside.

2. Heat oil in a deep heavy pan, add cumin seeds, bay leaves, green cardamoms and black cardamoms, cinnamon and cloves. Stir. Add the ginger-garlic-chilli paste and saute.

3. Add kathal and stir, add coriander powder, salt and ground biryani masala. Add most of the fried onions, reserving a few for top. Add 5 cups of water and bring to boil.

4. Add the rice and mint. (If you like, now you can transfer rice to a rice cooker as this biryani cooks well in a rice cooker). Cook on low heat till all the water has been absorbed.

5. Now sprinkle milk in which saffron and kewra are soaked. Close the lid again. Serve hot garnished with fried onions. Serve with onion, tomato and mint raita.

Note: Grind 1 star anise (*phool chakri*), ¼ nutmeg (*jaiphal*) and 1 flower of mace (*javitri*) together to make biryani masala. Store the excess in a bottle. You can buy ready-made biryani masala too.

APRICOT PEACH BISCOTTI

Mousse topped on biscuits on a bed of apricot sauce.

Serves 10-12

200 gms fresh thick cream, 1½ cups apricot - peach juice (real active beverage)
3 tbsp sugar or to taste, 5 tsp gelatine soaked in ¾ cup apricot - peach juice
12 marie biscuits or digestive biscuits, 250 gm black grapes

SAUCE
2½ cups apricot - peach juice, 2 tbsp sugar, 3 tbsp cornflour

DECORATION
a few tinned cherries, a few tiny basil or mint leaves

1. Beat cream in a bowl till fluffy and soft peaks form.

2. In a clean pan mix juice and sugar. Keep on fire and bring to a boil. Stir to dissolve sugar. Remove from fire. Keep aside.

3. Soak gelatine in ¾ cup juice for 10 minutes. Heat on slow fire to dissolve it completely. Gradually add the hot gelatine into the warm juice, stirring continuously.

4. Mix some cream into the gelatine-juice mixture. Add this mix slowly into the remaining whipped cream stirring nicely. Pour into a dish. Refrigerate for 4-5 hours for the mousse to set.

5. For the sauce, mix all ingredients and cook till you get a sauce of coating consistency. Pour sauce in a big low sided dish which can accommodate 10-12 biscuits at the bottom of the dish. Immediately arrange biscuits on the hot sauce, keeping 1" gap between the biscuits.

6. Arrange 2 grapes, each cut into 2 pieces lengthwise at 4 points on the biscuit. Top with a scoop of mousse. Cut very thin slices of a grape. Place 2 slices upright with some space in between on the scoop. Arrange a cherry and a tiny green leaf to complete the garnish. Refrigerate till serving, but 2-3 hours before serving, put in the freezer to get really cold before serving.

MANGO CHEESE CAKE

Serves 8

BASE
100 gms pack digestive biscuit, 5 tsp melted butter

CHEESE CAKE
1 cup milk

½ cup condensed milk

1 tbsp cornflour

2 cups of thick yogurt - hang for 30 minutes to get 1 cup hung yogurt

200 gms paneer - grated (2 cups)

2 cups mango puree, ½ cup powdered sugar

4 tsp gelatine - soaked in ¼ cup mango juice

TOPPING
1 tsp gelatine soaked in ¾ cup mango juice or ½ packet mango jelly

1. Mix milk, condensed milk and cornflour in a deep pan. Keep on fire and stirring continuously bring to a boil. Remove from fire and let it cool.

2. Place paneer, hung yogurt, mango puree and sugar in a blender. Blend to a very smooth paste. Add the mixture to the above milk mixture.

3. Soak 4 tsp gelatine in ¼ cup mango juice. Stir on low heat till gelatine dissolves. Add 1 tbsp yogurt mixture into the gelatine and mix well. Gradually add 2-3 tbsp more yogurt mixture into gelatine, mixing well. Now add the gelatine mix into the remaining yogurt mixture. Mix well

4. For the base, place broken biscuit in a dry blender and pour melted butter on it. Blend to get fine crumbs. Transfer the crumbs to a loose bottom cake tin or a cheese cake tin (8" diameter) and press with finger tips. Place the tin in the freezer for 10 minutes to set.

5. To assemble, pour the cheese cake mixture on the set base. Cover and place in the fridge (not freezer) for 4-5 hours till set.

6. For the topping, soak gelatine in the juice, stir on low heat till dissolved. Keep aside to cool slightly. When no longer hot, pour over the set cheese cake. Roll the tin to spread the topping evenly. Place in the fridge again to set the topping. Decorate with kiwi and mango slices.

PISTA LIME RING

Serves 8-10

3 tbsp semolina (*suji*), 2 cups milk, ½ cup sugar
4 tsp gelatine soaked in ¼ cup orange juice
400 ml (2 cups) cream
3 tbsp pistas or almonds (15-20) - blanched and ground to a paste with ¼ cup milk
2 drops vanilla essence, a drop of green colour, rind of 1 lemon

DECORATE
1 tbsp pista - blanched and chopped finely

1. Soak gelatine in juice for 5 minutes. Stir gelatine on low heat till you get a clear mixture. Do not boil. Leave aside. Keep the ring mould in the freezer to chill.
2. Warm the milk & sugar in a deep pan and stir till sugar dissolves. Do not boil.
3. Sprinkle the semolina on the milk. Mix well and bring to a boil. Simmer on low heat for 5 minutes, stirring constantly till thickened. Add the almond or pista paste and stir for a minute. Remove from heat.
4. Add gelatine mixture to the semolina and mix well.
5. Whip cream with essence till thick and fluffy. Fold 2 tbsp cream into the semolina mix. Add the remaining cream. Add lemon rind. Mix well and check taste. Pour into a chilled ring mould and refrigerate for 4-6 hours to set. To serve, run a knife around the inside & the outside rings & invert on the platter. If you like, fill the centre with fresh or tinned fruits. Decorate with chopped pista.

BAKED YOGURT WITH SPICED FIGS

Serves 4-6

YOGURT MIX
125 gms yogurt (curd), 100 gms cream, 100 gms condensed milk (¼ tin)

SPICED FIGS
100 gms (8-10 pieces) dry figs (*anjeer*), 100 ml (½ cup) grape juice, 2 tsp sugar
1" cinnamon (dalchini) stick, 3-4 cloves (laung), 2-3 pepper corns (saboot kali mirch)

1. Beat yogurt, cream and condensed milk together with a beater till smooth. Pour in an oven proof serving dish. Heat oven to 130°C. Bake dessert for 8 minutes till set. Chill
2. For the spiced figs, place all the ingredients in a pan and boil for 3-4 minutes on low heat. Cover and leave for 30 minutes, for the flavours to blend well. Serve cold with chilled yogurt.

MOCHA SYRUP PUDDING

1¼ cups plain flour, ½ cup cocoa powder, 1 tsp baking powder, ½ tsp soda-bi-carb
¾ cup yogurt (use fresh home made curd), 1 cup powdered sugar
½ cup oil
3 tsp coffee powder mixed in 1 tbsp hot water, 1 tsp vanilla essence
a big ring mould (8" diameter)

COFFEE SYRUP
3 tsp coffee powder, ¾ cup brown sugar, 1 cup water

FRUIT CREAM TO FILL
½ cup thick cream, 2 tbsp powdered sugar, or to taste
1 cup fruit cocktail - strain to discard liquid and leave in the strainer for 15 minutes
1 tbsp black raisins
2 tbsp chopped almonds and 2 tbsp chopped cashews - toasted on a *tawa* till golden

1. Grease a big (8-9" diameter) ring tin with oil, using a brush.

2. Sift flour, baking powder and cocoa powder together.

3. Combine coffee and hot water.

4. Beat yogurt and sugar till thick. Add coffee mix and essence.

5. Add oil very gradually, while beating continuously.

6. Fold in sifted flour mixture with wooden spoon gently.

7. Pour mixture into tin. Bake in preheated oven at 160°C/325°F for 45-50 minutes. Insert a skewer or knife to check cake. After 5 minutes, remove cake from tin to a wire rack.

8. For the coffee syrup, combine water & brown sugar and bring to a boil. Simmer for 2-3 minutes. Add coffee, stir over low heat to mix well. Remove from fire. Transfer the cake to a serving platter. Spoon hot syrup over the hot over cake.

9. Let the cake absorb the syrup. Keep aside. After it cools, cover with a wrap or invert the empty cake ring tin on the cake to prevent it from drying. You can leave it outside the fridge if it has to be served on the same day or refrigerate.

10. To make fruit cream, whip cream till very stiff. If using tatra pack cream, take only thick cream, discarding the liquid. Whip till thick. Add 2 tbsp powdered sugar and ¼ tsp vanilla essence to whipped cream and whip till stiff. Add fruit cocktail, toasted nuts & raisins to whipped cream. Refrigerate till serving time.

11. To serve the pudding, warm the cake for 5-10 seconds in the microwave to bring it to room temperature. Fill the centre hollow with fruit cream to give a heaped look. Serve.

FRIED ICE CREAM BALL

A wonderful combination of hot and cold. Remember to use a well set, hard ice cream for this dessert. Should be made well in advance, so that it is firm at the time of frying.

Serves 8

1 hard family brick (1 lt) vanilla ice cream - scooped to make big balls, about 7-8
10-12 slices of fresh bread - broken into small pieces
5 tbsp orange marmalade or any other jam, ¾ cup desiccated coconut (coconut powder)

COATING
½ cup rice flour mixed with about 1/3 cup water to make a paste

1. Grind half of the bread at a time in the mixer to get bread crumbs. Remove from mixer to a big bowl. Grind the remaining bread and put all in the bowl.

2. To the bread crumbs, add jam and coconut powder. Mix gently.

3. Take a scoop of ice cream and make it into a round ball by rolling it between your hands. Immediately put in the bread bowl and picking up the bread crumbs, coat the ball nicely with bread to absorb the melting ice cream. Keep in the freezer for 1 hour.

4. Put rice flour in a separate bowl. Add water to get a thin pouring consistency. Roll the hardened ice cream ball in rice flour paste. Keep in the freezer in a bread box till serving time.

5. At serving time, heat 1½ cups oil in a *kadhai* for frying. Do not fill the *kadhai* with too much oil. Put one ball at a time in hot oil. Change side after 30 seconds. Do not touch it immediately. Fry turning sides till crisp and golden. Remove on paper napkins to absorb excess oil. Serve whole or cut into half with a sharp knife. Top with a little coconut powder if you like.

CHOCOLATE CHEESE CAKE CUPS

Serves 6

6 choco chip biscuits
200 gms cream, a few drops vanilla essence
4 tbsp powdered sugar, 100 gms paneer -grated, ½ cup thick yogurt
200 gms dark chocolate - cut into small pieces
½ cup toasted walnuts - crushed coarsely

GARNISH
25 gms chocolate - grated on the biggest holes to get tiny curls

1. Crush the biscuits coarsely, divide the crushed biscuits evenly between 6 flat based glasses.
2. Whip the cream with vanilla essence and sugar till light.
3. Blend the paneer and yogurt in a small blender till smooth.
4. Heat the chopped chocolate over hot water (a double boiler) till softened. Remove the bowl from hot water and beat the chocolate till smooth & melted.
5. Fold cream in small batches into the melted chocolate and mix well.
6. Now add the paneer, yogurt mixture and ½ of the crushed walnuts.
7. Pour over the crushed biscuits and decorate with the remaining walnuts and grated chocolate. Refrigerate for 2-3 hours to chill.

APRICOT DELIGHT

Serves 4-6

1 cup (125 gms) dried apricots (*khurmani*)
250 gms (1 cup) fresh yogurt, 200 ml (1 cup) cream
6-8 tbsp powdered sugar, 1 orange

1. Soak the apricots in water for 3-4 hours till soft.
2. Remove the stones and blend the apricots to a puree.
3. Break and remove the almond or kernel from the stones and keep aside.
4. Hang the yogurt for 15 minutes in a muslin cloth. To remove excess water gently press the muslin cloth to get a thick yogurt.
5. Place the yogurt in a bowl and beat well, add cream and sugar and beat again to get a smooth mixture, add the apricot puree and mix well.
6. Pour the mixture in a glass bowl, remove the skin and seeds from the almonds.
7. Garnish the pudding with orange segments & the apricot almonds. Serve chilled.

GAJAR KI TUKDI

Makes 15

PANCAKES
½ cup plain flour (*maida*), ¾-1 cup milk, approx.
½ tsp cinnamon powder, a big pinch of baking powder (1/8 tsp)

CARROT FILLING
250 gms carrots - grated finely, 1 cup milk, 2 tbsp milk powder, 2½ tbsp sugar
seeds of 3 green cardamoms (*chhoti illaichi*) - crushed, 6-8 almonds-crushed
1½ tbsp ghee

PANEER FILLING
200 gms paneer grated finely, ½ tsp ghee
2½ tbsp sugar, 2 tbsp pistachio (*pistas*) - chopped and crushed
few strands of saffron (*kesar*), ¼ tsp green cardamom (*chhoti illaichi*) powder

TO SERVE
thin rabri (made from ½ litre milk + 1 tbsp sugar), few chopped pistachio

1. Mix flour and cinnamon powder. Add enough milk and stir to get a batter of a thin pouring consistency. Keep aside for 15-20 minutes.

2. Add baking powder and mix well. Grease a non stick pan with little ghee. Keep on fire to heat the pan. Remove pan from fire and pour some batter. Quickly swirl the pan to cover the base. Cook the pancakes on low flame till well cooked. Remove pancakes to a greased plate.

3. For the carrot filling, put the grated carrots in a non stick pan on medium heat for about 5 minutes till the moisture from the carrots has dried up. Add milk and simmer for 5-7 minutes till liquid evaporates. Add milk powder, sugar, cardamoms and crushed almonds. Add ghee and saute well for another 5-7 minutes till dry. Remove from heat. Cool.

4. For the paneer filling, put the crumbled paneer in a non stick pan add ghee, saute on low heat for 2 minutes. Add sugar, saffron and crushed pistachio. Remove from heat.

5. To assemble, place a pancake on a flat surface, spread carrot filling evenly on the pancake, over it spread the paneer filling. Roll the pancake tightly. Place in the freezer compartment of the fridge for 1 hour. Remove from freezer and cut diagonally into 1½ inch thick slices. Place them in the serving platter and drizzle some thin rabri on them. Serve garnished with chopped pistachio.

Note: If the pancake is under cooked, it will break while rolling. You can make the rolls a day in advance. Cut them at serving time.

FRUIT PIZZA

Serves 6-8

BASE
¼ cup (40 gms) butter
¼ cup powdered sugar, 1 tbsp brown sugar
¾ cup maida (plain flour), ½ tsp baking soda, ¼ tsp baking powder
40 ml (3-4 tbsp) milk, ¼ tsp vanilla essence

FILLING
200 gms yogurt - hang for 15 minutes only, ½ cup powdered sugar
150 gms thick cream, ½ tsp vanilla essence, 1½ tbsp gelatine - soaked in 4 tbsp water

ORANGE SAUCE
½ cup ready-made orange juice, 2 tbsp sugar
1 tbsp lemon juice, ¼ tsp lemon rind, ¼ tsp orange rind
2 tsp cornflour mixed in 2 tbsp orange juice

FRESH FRUITS
kiwi, anaar, bananas, apples, oranges, strawberries and grapes

1. Preheat the oven to 180°C/350°F. Grease and dust an 8" pizza pan or a big baking tray or an oven proof glass pie dish.

2. To prepare the base, mix butter, sugar and brown sugar till light.

3. Sift together flour, baking soda and baking powder. Add this to the butter-sugar mixture. Add milk and vanilla essence. Mix well. Knead very well, beating the dough on the kitchen platform a number of times to get a smooth firm dough.

4. Make a ball of the dough and flatten lightly. Place the dough in the greased baking tray and pat it evenly to thin round pizza base, about 7-8" diameter. Bake for 15 minutes till golden brown. Cool.

5. For the filling, squeeze excess water from the hung yogurt. Beat it with sugar till smooth. Add cream and essence and beat well. Heat the soaked gelatine slightly till it dissolves. Add 1 tbsp yogurt-cream to dissolved gelatine and mix well. Add 2-3 tbsp more yogurt to gelatine and mix. Now add the gelatine to the filling mixture. Spread yogurt over the cooled crust, leaving a little of the edges showing.

6. Make thin slices of all the fruits. Place the fruits decoratively on the set filling covering the whole pizza.

7. For the sauce, mix all the ingredients of the sauce and cook on low heat till it thickens. Let it cool. Pour the cooled sauce over it to form a glaze. Place in the fridge to set. Chill until ready to serve.

SHAHI KESARI PANEER

Makes 16

8 slices of bread
5 tbsp of chopped mixed nuts (almond, raisin, pistachio etc.)
¾ cup cold milk

PANEER LAYER

3 cups milk
½ cup sugar, ¼ tsp saffron (*kesar*)
seeds of 6 green cardamoms (*chhoti illaichi*) - powdered
5 tbsp custard powder dissolved in ½ cup milk
100 gm cottage cheese (*paneer*) - grated
2 drops of *kewra* essence

TO DECORATE

silver sheet (*vark*), mixed chopped nuts

1. Boil sugar with ½ cup water and saffron in a separate pan. Keep on low heat for 5 minutes. Add grated cottage cheese. Cook for only 1 minute. Remove from fire and keep aside.

2. Boil 3 cups milk. Give 2-3 boils. Add custard paste to the milk, stirring continuously. Keep stirring for 2 minutes till thick.

3. Add the prepared sugar and paneer mixture. Boil. Keep on heat for 1 minute. Remove from fire. Cool. Add kewra essence. Sprinkle cardamom powder.

4. Remove the side crusts of bread. Cut each slice into 4 square pieces. Heat oil in a *kadhai*. Deep fry bread tukdis in 3-4 batches on medium heat till golden brown. Remove from oil on a paper napkin. Let it cool.

5. Take a serving dish. Spread half of the kesari paneer in the dish.

6. Dip each piece of bread for a second in ¾ cup cold milk, kept in a small bowl. Remove bread immediately.

7. Spread about 1 tsp of the paneer mixture on each piece of bread. Place in the dish. Sprinkle 1 tsp of chopped mixed nuts on the bread. Dip another piece of bread in milk and place over the bread covered with nuts in the dish. Press lightly. Make 16 sandwiched tukdis in the same way and arrange in the dish.

8. Cover each tukdi with the remaining paneer mixture. Decorate with silver sheet and nuts. Cover with a cling wrap (plastic film) and let it set for at least 1 hour before serving. Serve at room temperature or cold.

ICE CREAM CHARLOTTE

Serves 8

2 packs of sliced fruit cake

1 litre butter scotch ice cream and 500 ml vanilla/strawberry ice cream

2-3 tbsp strawberry crush

2 tbsp raisins (*kishmish*)

4-5 oreo or any dark chocolate cookies - broken into pieces and frozen for 30 minutes or more

PRALINE & CARAMELIZED SHARTS FOR DECORATION

1 cup regular sugar

a small flat pan, oil for greasing

2 tbsp chopped almonds

1. To assemble the charlotte, arrange cake slices around the edges of a 9" loose bottom cake tin. Now arrange slices on the bottom of the tin which will keep the side slices in place. Pour 2-3 tbsp crush on the bottom slices and spread with a spoon.

2. Put slices of both the ice creams alternately on the cake. Sprinkle raisins and cookies on the ice cream and push them in lightly. Level the height of the ice cream with the height of the cake on the edges. Cover with foil. Put a plate on it and put in the freezer for 6-8 hours or preferably overnight to set.

3. For the praline topping and decoration, grease the kitchen platform with some oil. Put ½ cup sugar in a small flat pan or a non stick pan. Spread out in a flat layer covering the bottom of the pan. Keep on medium heat for 2-3 minutes without touching the sugar. When the sugar starts to turn golden at the edges, reduce heat and rotate the pan gently. Wait till it turns light golden. Do not make it too golden. Immediately, with a spoon pour out leaves or abstract design on the greased platform, keeping a hole in the centre of the shart.

4. To make praline, caramelize the remaining ½ cup sugar till golden in the same way. Remove from fire. Add nuts to the caramel. Pour on the greased platform. Let them cool. Gently remove from the platform and crush to a coarse powder.

5. 2-3 hours before serving take out the cake on a big enough serving platter. Sprinkle the praline powder to cover. Decorate with caramel sharts in between the cake slices and in the centre. Keep in the freezer till serving time.

Note: Store caramel sharts and powder outside the fridge in air tight containers.

CHOCO WEB PIE

For a good short crust base it is important to chill the unbaked crust in the freezer for 10-15 minutes and then put in the hot oven. The pastry is much lighter this way.

Makes 16 thin pieces

SHORT CRUST
150 gm (1½ cups) flour (*maida*), 5 bread slices - ground to fresh crumbs (2½ cups)
100 gm butter - cut into pieces and keep in the fridge to chill, 3 tbsp powdered sugar

CARAMEL NUT FILLING
1 cup roasted peanuts
½ cup chopped almonds & ½ cup raisins - roasted together for 3 minutes on a *tawa*
1¼ cups sugar (regular) + 1/3 cup water, ¾ cup cream - at room temperature

TOP GANACHE TOPPING
200 gm chocolate, 150 gm cream (¾ cup), 1 tbsp rum (optional)

TO DECORATE
a toothpick, 8-10 almonds - halved, some grated chocolate curls

1. Put cold butter in a mixer with sugar and churn for a few seconds. Add flour and fresh bread crumbs to the mixer and run mixer for a few seconds till crumbly. Remove from mixer. Bind mixture and mix gently into a dough of rolling consistency. Wrap in a cling wrap. Keep aside for 30 minutes in the fridge.

2. Grease a 8-9" flan tin or pie tin. Roll out a large chappati, larger than the tin so as to cover the sides too, of 1/8" thickness between 2 sheets of polythene and place in the flan tin. Prick with a fork. Keep in the freezer for 10 minutes. Bake blind for 20 minutes at 200°C/400°F till light golden. Let it cool.

3. For the caramel nut topping, put 1¼ cups sugar in a clean heavy bottom pan in a thin layer. Let it turn golden on the edges without stirring. Reduce heat. Rotate pan to melt sugar and turn golden. Add 1/3 cup warm water and stir continuously with a spoon to dissolve the lump. Do not lift the lumpy spoon from the pan as the caramelized sugar turns hard and it becomes difficult to dissolve the lump. Keep stirring with the spoon till smooth.

4. Add cream. Immediately remove from fire and stir to mix well. Add nuts. Mix well. Fill nuts into the baked pie crust or shell.

5. For the topping ganache, warm cream on low heat in a heavy pan for 1 minute. Add chocolate. Mix well. Remove from heat and stir well to get a smooth ganache. Add 1 tbsp rum. Mix. Pour over the nuts to cover completely.

6. Refrigerate for 1-2 hours to set. Mark circles with a tooth pick at ½" gaps. Similarly, mark lines across the pie at ½" distance. Arrange almonds and curls on the pie. Serve pie cold or at room temperature.

MANGO AMBROSIA

Fruits in mango sauce. You can serve this in individual cups also.

Serves 4-6

2 cups chopped mango (fresh or tinned) or 2 cups tinned mango pulp
seeds of 8 green cardamoms (*chhoti illaichi*) - crushed
½ cup mango juice
½ cup cream
2 tbsp powdered sugar
2½ cups chopped fruits (apple, grape, pomegranate, banana, pineapple, chickoo)

GARNISH

few pomegranate kernels (*anaar ke dane*)
silver sheet (*vark*)
soaked and chopped almonds and pistachios

1. Place the chopped mangoes, cardamon seeds, juice and sugar in a mixer. Blend to a smooth sauce, add the cream and blend again to get a sauce of a thick pouring consistency.

2. Place chopped fruits in a flat serving dish. Pour the mango sauce over the fruits. Cover and chill.

3. Garnish with pomegranate, vark and nuts. Serve cold.

INTERNATIONAL CONVERSION GUIDE

These are not exact equivalents; they've been rounded-off to make measuring easier.

WEIGHTS & MEASURES

METRIC	IMPERIAL
15 g	½ oz
30 g	1 oz
60 g	2 oz
90 g	3 oz
125 g	4 oz (¼ lb)
155 g	5 oz
185 g	6 oz
220 g	7 oz
250 g	8 oz (½ lb)
280 g	9 oz
315 g	10 oz
345 g	11 oz
375 g	12 oz (¾ lb)
410 g	13 oz
440 g	14 oz
470 g	15 oz
500 g	16 oz (1 lb)
750 g	24 oz (1½ lb)
1 kg	30 oz (2 lb)

LIQUID MEASURES

METRIC	IMPERIAL
30 ml	1 fluid oz
60 ml	2 fluid oz
100 ml	3 fluid oz
125 ml	4 fluid oz
150 ml	5 fluid oz (¼ pint/1 gill)
190 ml	6 fluid oz
250 ml	8 fluid oz
300 ml	10 fluid oz (½ pint)
500 ml	16 fluid oz
600 ml	20 fluid oz (1 pint)
1000 ml	1¾ pints

CUPS & SPOON MEASURES

METRIC	IMPERIAL
1 ml	¼ tsp
2 ml	½ tsp
5 ml	1 tsp
15 ml	1 tbsp
60 ml	¼ cup
125 ml	½ cup
250 ml	1 cup

HELPFUL MEASURES

METRIC	IMPERIAL
3 mm	1/8 in
6 mm	¼ in
1 cm	½ in
2 cm	¾ in
2.5 cm	1 in
5 cm	2 in
6 cm	2½ in
8 cm	3 in
10 cm	4 in
13 cm	5 in
15 cm	6 in
18 cm	7 in
20 cm	8 in
23 cm	9 in
25 cm	10 in
28 cm	11 in
30 cm	12 in (1ft)

HOW TO MEASURE

When using the graduated metric measuring cups, it is important to shake the dry ingredients loosely into the required cup. Do not tap the cup on the table, or pack the ingredients into the cup unless otherwise directed. Level top of cup with a knife. When using graduated metric measuring spoons, level top of spoon with a knife. When measuring liquids in the jug, place jug on a flat surface, check for accuracy at eye level.

OVEN TEMPERATURE

These oven temperatures are only a guide. Always check the manufacturer's manual.

	°C (Celsius)	°F (Fahrenheit)	Gas Mark
Very low	120	250	1
Low	150	300	2
Moderately low	160	325	3
Moderate	180	350	4
Moderately high	190	375	5
High	200	400	6
Very high	230	450	7

GLOSSARY OF NAMES/TERMS

Appetizers	Small tasty bits of food served before meals.
Aubergine	Brinjal/eggplant
Au gratin	Any dish made with white sauce and covered with cheese and then baked or grilled.
Baste	To brush the food with some fat during cooking in the oven, to keep it moist and soft.
Batter	Any mixture of flour and a liquid which is beaten or stirred to make a pouring consistency.
Bell peppers	Capsicums
Blanch	To remove skin by dipping into hot water for a couple of minutes. e.g. to blanch tomatoes or almonds.
Brinjal	Aubergine/eggplant
Brussle sprouts	Baby cabbage
Cilantro	Coriander
Cornstarch	Cornflour
Coriander	Cilantro
Curry powder	A blend of Indian spices.
Desiccated coconut	Powdered coconut.
Dice	To cut into small neat cubes.
Dot	To put small amounts.
Dough	A mixture of flour, liquid etc., kneaded together into a stiff paste or roll.
Drain	To remove liquid from food.
Green beans	French beans
Marinate	To soak food in a mixture for some time so that the flavour of the mixture penetrates into the food.
Minced	Very finely chopped.
Okra	A green vegetable, also called lady finger.
Plain flour	All purpose flour, *maida*.
Puree	A smooth mixture obtained by rubbing cooked vegetables or blanched tomatoes through a sieve.
Saute	To toss and make light brown in shallow fat.
Soup cubes	Flavourful cubes added to soups or sauces. Also called seasoning cubes or stock cubes.
Tofu	Cheese prepared by curdling soya bean milk.
Turmeric	A yellow spice with antiseptic properties. Usually available as a powder. It imparts a yellow colour to food.

Nita Mehta's New Cookbook Series @ Rs. 99/- Only

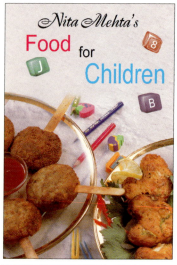

Nita Mehta's **Food** for **Children**

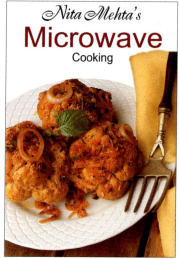

Nita Mehta's **Microwave** Cooking

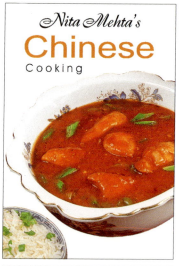

Nita Mehta's **Chinese** Cooking

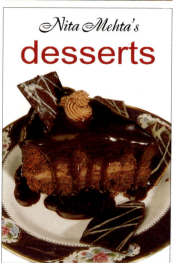

Nita Mehta's **desserts**

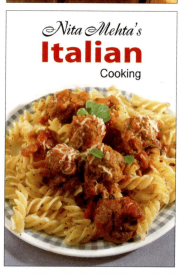

Nita Mehta's **Italian** Cooking

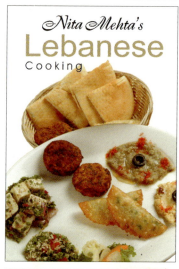

Nita Mehta's **Lebanese** Cooking

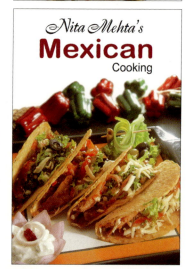

Nita Mehta's **Mexican** Cooking

Nita Mehta's **Soups & Salads**

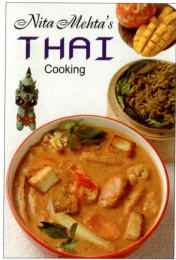

Nita Mehta's **THAI** Cooking

BIG SIZE, ALL COLOUR, PAPERBACK

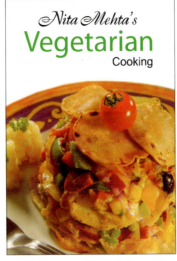
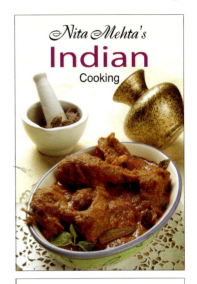
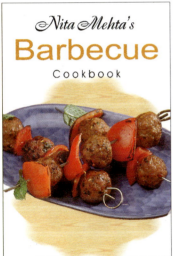
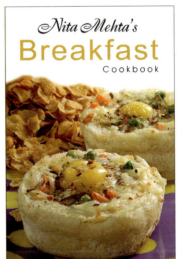

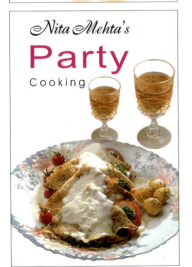

BEST SELLERS BY *Nita Mehta*

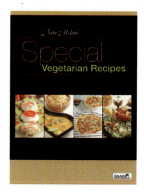

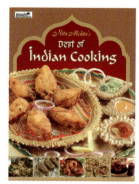

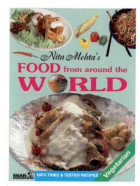

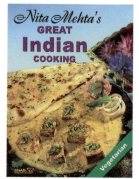

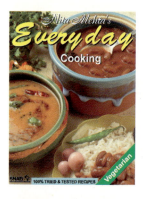

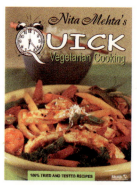

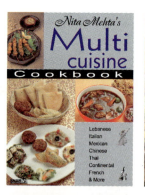

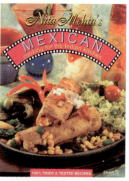

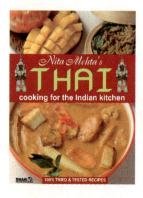

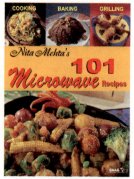

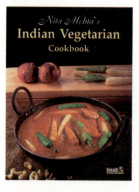

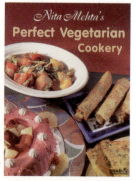

Children Books by

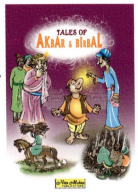

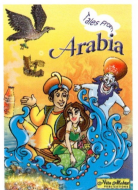
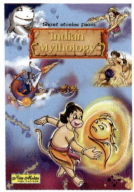
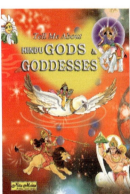
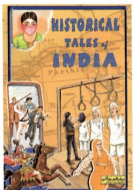
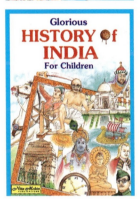
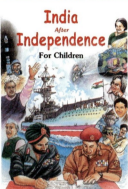
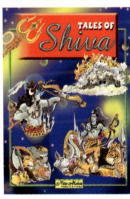
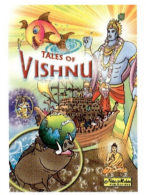
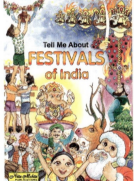
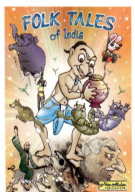
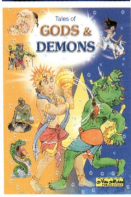
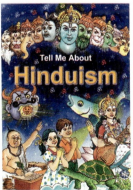
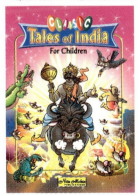
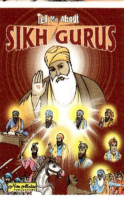